MW01251472

MENTAL
MALPRACTICE

MENTAL MALPRACTICE

Protecting the mind from
hypnotic influence through
prayer in Christian Science

ANN BEALS

The Bookmark
Santa Clarita, California

Library of Congress Control Number: 2001119339

Beals, Ann.
    Mental malpractice : protecting the mind from
    hypnotic influence through prayer in Christian Science /
Ann Beals.
        p. cm.
        ISBN 0-930227-32-8

    1. Christian Science. 2. Brainwashing. 3. Hypnotic
susceptibility. 4. Prayer.   I. Title.

BX6943.1343 2002   289.5
                                QBI33-205

Published by
The Bookmark
Post Office Box 801143
Santa Clarita, California 91380

BY THE AUTHOR:

Scientific Prayer
Christian Science Treatment: The Prayer that Heals
Introduction to Christian Science
Animal Magnetism
Christian Science and the Threat of Mind Control
The Law of Love
The Secret Place: How to Find Your Oneness with God
The Spiritual Dimension
Crisis in The Christian Science Church

CONTENTS

INTRODUCTION

In this century, the hidden use of mental power to control or harm the unsuspecting mind, has become general knowledge. Never before in the history of the Western World, has mind control been understood and practiced so widely and in so many subtle and devious ways as in the present day. The practice of the most malicious forms of hypnotism — occultism, voodoo, witchcraft, black magic and Satanism — is on the rise. The abuse of mental power has become so subtle and sophisticated that the average mind is the target of aggressive mental suggestion in all areas of his daily life.

Those who would never consider abusing the mind's power, must now have a way of defending themselves from hypnotic influence. Such protection must be mental in nature, for hypnotism is a mental force. It works silently, secretly, reaching through walls and over vast distances. There are no physical barriers to protect one from its influence, nor does human goodness and blind faith in God sufficiently shield the innocent mind.

The purpose of this book is to show that an understanding of Christian Science provides a refuge from mental malpractice and successfully protects the mind from all forms of hypnotism. This protection comes as we define the many ways that hypnotic influence can be exercised over the mind, and learn how prayer in Christian Science enables us to be immune to such control.

My discussion on this subject is not based on research into hypnosis and mind control. I have no knowledge of how to hypnotize. But through the study of Christian Science, I have learned how to recognize malpractice, and successfully defend the mind from even the most malicious mental attacks. I am not writing about how hypnotism works, but how it is possible to recognize and prevent its harmful effects.

This subject is not new to Christian Science. Mary Baker Eddy, the Discoverer and Founder of Christian Science, tried to impress on her students again and again the need to defend themselves against malicious malpractice. Early in her mission, she learned the difference between the harmful effects of hypnotism and the protective power of scientific prayer. During the Victorian Age, the threat of hypnotic control was not yet universally recognized. When Mrs. Eddy tried to warn her early students of the urgent need to defend themselves against malpractice, the students did not understand the value of her teachings. Some became terrified of malpractice, while others felt that she was a fanatic on the subject. A few students perverted her teachings, and malpracticed against her and her students. She came to realize the need to be more cautious in instructing others about secret hypnosis, but she never stopped warning her trusted students of the need to handle malpractice.

After she passed on in 1910, the subject of malpractice gradually faded out of Christian Science teaching. To read the material published by the Christian Science Church today, one would never know that Mrs. Eddy taught so prolifically, so intensely, and so wisely, on the handling of malpractice. This teaching has become non-existent within the organization, and Christian Scientists have been led to believe that handling malpractice is no longer necessary. When we consider the phenomenal success of the Christian Science Church when Mrs. Eddy was teaching on malpractice, in contrast to its unchecked decline today, this should indicate that handling malpractice is still an urgent need.

For myself, many suffering experiences have taught me to take malpractice very seriously. I have great respect for the painful, dulling, disastrous effects it has on the mind. I have learned the dire necessity of knowing what it is, and how it operates. An understanding of malpractice is absolutely essential to anyone striving to demonstrate the whole of Christian Science.

It is not my purpose to frighten you about malpractice, but to enlighten you. Please consider the fact that, as you read this, you probably have given little thought to the workings of malpractice. How often are you an innocent victim of it? Isn't it better to be informed and capable of handling its harmful influence, than to suffer from it? Simply to be aware of how malpractice operates, can be enough to prevent it from doing so. Few Scientists today realize how often malpractice stops them from going deeper into Christian Science, or it can cause a seemingly incurable or recurring physical illness, or it can reverse our demonstrations.

This is the darkest, most negative aspect of Christian Science that we must explore, because in so doing we must take into account not only our own mortal thoughts and emotions, but those of others. When the subject of malpractice is mentioned to a good and moral person, he usually finds it difficult — even impossible — to accept the fact that someone would intentionally try to harm or destroy him through malicious mental attacks. The work of such a godless mentality is so foreign to his nature that he cannot conceive of it. Such a naivete leaves him totally undefended against malpractice, and he can suffer severely from such mental work.

There are others who have been led to believe that they do not need to handle malpractice. They will say that Mrs. Eddy's concern for it was only for her time. But be assured that the hypnotic work of the antichrist is as aggressive today as it has ever been. It comes from many undefined sources and works in many unexpected ways. Therefore, we must be willing to examine this activity of evil in order to understand it, for this alone will give us dominion over it.

It is reassuring to know that we do not spend eternity handling malicious malpractice. This is a phase of our work in Christian Science that we pass through. We begin by learning to detect the workings of malpractice and its intrusion into the consciousness, then we demonstrate the ability to protect consciousness from its harmful influence, and lastly we go beyond its reach. Such spiritual lessons are not to be avoided, but welcomed as important milestones in learning to overcome animal magnetism.

It is in Christian Science that we find a haven from malpractice, for it enables us to separate God's thoughts from hypnotic suggestions, and to handle malpractice with assurance. In so doing, we find a refuge from the antichrist.

It is my fondest hope that this discussion on malpractice will give the reader a sound basis for freeing and protecting his mind from the influence of evil suggestions, that he will find an escape from the aggressive mental suggestions that are increasing daily, and learn to rest in the gentle presence of divine Love.

Ann Beals
2001

Quotations from Mrs. Eddy's published and unpublished writings are given, along with other references and recommended reading, at the end of each section or chapter. Where quotations by Mrs. Eddy are given, the following abbreviations are used:

> *Science and Health* - S&H
> *Miscellaneous Writings* - Mis
> *Message to The Mother Church for 1901* - '01
> *The First Church of Christ, Scientist and Miscellany* - My
> *Divinity Course and General Collectanea* - DC

Chapter I

THE UNIVERSAL THREAT
OF MIND CONTROL

As the world moves into a mental age, there is no greater threat to man's freedom and well being than the modern day knowledge of mind control. Secret mental malpractice, brainwashing, subliminal suggestion, aggressive mental suggestion, mental manipulation, occultism, witchcraft and black magic, practiced daily throughout the world, are a prolific source of human suffering. All have one common denominator — *hypnotism*. The malicious mental powers of one human mind directed toward another can be so aggressive as to destroy the victim spiritually, mentally, morally, and even physically, and this is now a generally accepted fact.

It was inevitable that man's progress would eventually lead to the discovery of the mind's ability to secretly hypnotize another. It was once assumed that one could not be hypnotized without his consent; but, in fact, one can be hypnotized without his consent or knowledge. The harmful, even lethal, effects of secret malicious hypnotism are becoming increasingly apparent. Trained hypnotists can secretly hypnotize without the victim being aware of the attack on his mind.

This silent mental influence ranges from the ignorant malpractice we encounter in our daily contacts with others to the violent forms of malpractice secretly performed by trained hypnotists. There is the practice of hypnosis in the medical and psychological fields, in scientific research and investigation. Knowledge of hypnotism has resulted in the attempt to influence and control

1

large populations through psycho-political warfare and the media. There is the growing practice in the Western world of occultism and Oriental hypnotism. As the focus of world thought shifts from the physical to the mental realm, the power of the mind is becoming known to millions.

Many forms of malpractice can come through subliminal suggestion, personal relationships, and collective world thought. One could say that the Western world is submerged in a whirlpool of aggressive mental suggestion.

The use of hypnotic control has become so widespread and effective, that should it continue to develop, the universal practice of such godless mental power could result in anarchy. Hypnotic methods have become so clever and so subtle, that even the most intelligent and astute mind can be influenced secretly without realizing that it has been manipulated and controlled.

Because the most depraved uses of hypnosis are so far removed from the personal experience of the average mind, we may be inclined to believe that malpractice has little relationship to our immediate life. It seems to belong to events where great power struggles are taking place, where cult leaders are controlling their followers, and hypnotism is being used in trying to cure illness. Although many of us will never encounter the most malicious forms of hypnosis, such as brain-washing, mental assassination and Satanism, we do experience subtle forms of malpractice that invade our lives daily, and unless we are aware of this, we come under their hypnotic influence.

Many kinds of malpractice take place in our personal lives that have never been recognized as such: the tendency to malpractice on one's self; the malpractice found in personal relationships; the collective malpractice of general world beliefs. These, combined with the hypnotism practiced by the scientific, military and medical world, the media, religions, and the occult, all bare witness to Mrs. Eddy's warning, "The mental field of work is at war."

Christian Science the One True Defense

The most frightening aspect of the development of hypnotic control, is that *there appears to be no way to counteract it.* A victim seems to have no means of defending himself from its powers, and we can be certain that those who practice hypnotism know this. Finding a way to prevent malicious malpractice from affecting one's mind has become imperative, for nothing in present-day science and technology guarantees escape from hypnotic control. There is nothing in religious, metaphysical, or philosophical writings that tell us specifically how to handle malpractice.

Only in Christian Science do we find the one true defense against all forms of hypnotism.

Christian Science was discovered by Mary Baker Eddy in 1866. Early in her work of establishing her Cause, she learned that the secret hypnotic work of a malpractitioner could control, and even destroy another. She urged many of her students to defend their minds from aggressive mental suggestion. The handling of malicious malpractice became an important part of her teaching and writings.

In the first edition of *Retrospection and Introspection*, she wrote, "I have seen a person, when under the effect of Hypnotism, obey the will of one who was neither present, nor known to be attempting any such influence over him. I doubted whether this effect could be produced without the consent of the person to be affected; but this doubt was removed when I witnessed with horror, a superinduced state of involuntary mesmerism.

"The methods of Animal Magnetism, especially its secret work, should be exposed. This alone can protect the people from a future Reign of Terror, far surpassing the error and terrorism of the Dark Ages. One has nothing to fear from this evil, if he is conscious of its claim and its presence, and, on the basis of Christian Science, understands its impotence. Animal Magnetism is the oppo-

3

site of Christian Science; and its effects on the senses is readily removed by the latter, if the cause of this effect is understood."

Considering the extensive use of hypnotism presently taking place, her prediction of "a future Reign of Terror" is quite prophetic.

Because malpractice is entirely mental, the mind's protection and defense must also be mental. Evil's threat to mental freedom has become so complex and aggressive, that the answer to it cannot be a simple prayer or formula for handling hypnosis. The study of Christian Science gives us an *advanced intelligence* that can counteract mental malpractice, and prevent it from influencing us. This Science opens up a new dimension of the mind. It is an education in divine metaphysics, and as one develops an understanding of it, he learns to detect and defend himself against harmful hypnotic influence.

When properly understood in the light of modern day science, Christian Science is both a religious and scientific discovery of the first magnitude. It goes beyond the present belief of man and the universe as purely material and mental. It accurately defines the nature of God as the only cause and creator, and shows that man and the universe are governed by divine intelligence and love, not by evil and matter. As one develops this advanced intelligence, he spiritualizes consciousness — that is, he thinks in a new or spiritual form of intelligence regarding God, man, and the universe. This spiritual understanding is the opposite of hypnotism, and since both cannot exist in the same mind at the same time, this advanced intelligence provides a protection from all forms of malpractice. Thus through Christian Science, one finds himself in control of his mind, and able to defend himself against malpractice.

The way through which we gain this dominion over evil is quite simple. It is comprised of the consecrated study of the written word in Christian Science, coupled with the prayer of affirmation and denial. Such prayerful work heals and protects us to the extent that we understand and practice it.

4

Hypnotic Epidemics

Only as we begin to experience the protection of Christian Science, do we appreciate what it can do for us. Too often in the media and through personal contacts, we become part of what might be termed hypnotic epidemics. Human opinion and advice, recent surveys and 'scientific' reports, unrelieved threats, cautions and fears, are poured forth daily into our world, causing a flood of human misery.

If an epidemic of flu is suggested often enough into a certain locality, it will collectively hypnotize the people into believing a flu epidemic is inevitable and this causes an epidemic.

If a recession is predicted by experts in books and newspapers, and forecast on television, it will hypnotize the people into believing and fearing an impending economic decline, and so possibly bring about one.

If relationships in the media constantly portray conflict, hate, deceit, lust, and so on, and such drama is absorbed collectively by society, the people will gradually be hypnotized into behaving in a similar vein.

It has already been proven that crime and violence on television and in the movies, has the effect of causing widespread crime. To what extent were potential criminals influenced by aggressive mental suggestions coming in the guise of entertainment?

We have no way of knowing at this early date how deeply entrenched are the hypnotic suggestions that pour forth into the world we live in. Therefore we cannot begin too soon developing the moral and spiritual powers that annul and destroy such hypnotic conditioning. Hypnotic epidemics, ebbing and flowing through modern day society, will cease as they are confronted by prayerful work in Christian Science. And so our work in learning to handle malpractice will not only protect our own minds, but will go forth to purify the mental atmosphere of the world around us. If collective hypnosis can claim to produce sickness, disease, crime, and lack, collective scientific prayer can certainly produce safety, health, freedom and abundance.

Christian Science does far more than protect the mind from hypnotic influence. But for our discussion here, we will focus on this one subject. We will discuss malpractice and scientific prayer more thoroughly further on. But first, we will consider a brief history of both hypnotism and Christian Science in order to understand how they are opposite states of mind.

References by Mary Baker Eddy relevant to this Chapter:

As named in Christian Science, animal magnetism or hypnotism is the specific term for error, or mortal mind. It is the false belief that mind is in matter, and is both evil and good; that evil is as real as good and more powerful. This belief has not one quality of Truth. It is either ignorant or malicious. The malicious form of hypnotism ultimates in moral idiocy. . . .
Christian Science goes to the bottom of mental action, and reveals the theodicy which indicates the rightness of all divine action, as the emanation of divine Mind, and the consequent wrongness of the opposite so-called action, — evil, occultism, necromancy, mesmerism, animal magnetism, hypnotism. (*Science and Health* 103, 104)

Unless malpractice is exposed by Christian Scientists, the world will be little benefited by Christian Science. (DC p 278)

M.A.M. [Malicious Animal Magnetism] extinguishes all that is humane in human nature and utterly obscures to mortal view whatever is Divine. (DC p 165)

Mesmerism is a lie about God and man. Malpractice is the activity of animal magnetism; its law is that we cannot detect it, and that we do not want to handle it. (DC p 90)

From *Science and Health*, Second Edition
(1878) Penal law must meet the hour when he who hates his neighbor, will have no need to enter his door, to destroy his peace and prosperity, to harm his health, or to demoralize his household ; for the evil mind will do this through mesmerism; and not in *propria persona* be seen committing the deed. This 'irresistible conflict' awaits us, and must be met first by law, and next by Science, or mesmerism that scourge of man, will leave nothing sacred as mind becomes conscious of its latent powers. The mesmeric power will attempt to gloat revenge, malice, avarice, etc., but it will rebound on itself, and send the perpetrator of the foulest crimes to 'his own place' ; while metaphysical science shall pour blessings on all. (Vol. II, p. 63) (DC p 141)

From *Science and Health*, Third Edition
(1881) The crimes committed mentally are drifting the age towards self-defence; we hope the method it adopts will be more humane than in periods past. The re-establishment of the Christian era, or the medieval period of metaphysics, will be one of moderation and peace; but the reinauguration of this period will be met with demonology, or the unlicensed cruelty of mortal mind, that will compel mankind to learn metaphysics for a refuge and defence. Then shall be fulfilled the Scripture, 'The wrath of man shall praise Thee, and the remainder thereof Thou shalt restrain'. (Vol. II, p. 45) (DC p 141)

See article by Mrs. Eddy on "Malicious Animal Magnetism" in *Divinity Course and General Collectanea*, page 149.

Electricity functions by a discharge from the positive to the negative pole. From this phenomenon we learn the nature of animal magnetism in its claim to be contagious, and to dart from one mortal thought to another. Hence our defence must lie in acknowledging this claim and then refuting it with the truth of being.

Once Mrs. Eddy asked a student the question: "Do you understand the handling of electrical poisoning? It is mental thought transference with malice behind it — with an intent to harm. Mortal mind sends its messages without wires. It is aggressive mental suggestion maliciously directed." (DC xiii)

Chapter II

CHRISTIAN SCIENCE
versus HYPNOTISM

Hypnotism is as old as civilization. It first appeared, in ancient times as priestcraft, necromancy, curses, hypnotic healing and false prophecy. With the dawn of Christianity, spiritual healing was an important part of the early Church. As this new religion spread over the Western World and it grew in popularity, many of the occult practices of the past became part of the rituals of the new religion and slowly deadened the spirituality that had been the source of its healing works. During the Dark Ages, it is likely that so-called faith-healing and the supernatural were due more to hypnotism than the power of prayer.

With the Renaissance, faith-healing began to leave the cloistered world of the Church, and take on a crude form of scientific theory. At the dawn of the Age of Reason, it was natural that this great awakening should include an investigation into the phenomena known as faith-healing. A few inquiring minds in Europe began forming theories about "magnetic healing." Because faith-healing was considered a supernatural phenomena, early theories about it still acknowledged the final cause to be the "Eternal Creative Spirit" of the universe, to which was ascribed the cure of all wounds and diseases.

This early effort to plumb the secrets of so-called faith-healing, brought about the first ray of light thrown on the machinations the human mind. Among the first to divorce hypnotic healing

9

from religion, was a Viennese physician, Friedrich Anton Mesmer. He explained mental cures as wholly due to the operation of a non-intelligent magnetic mechanical force. Drawing upon the theories of others, Mesmer formulated his own philosophy in which the spiritual element entirely disappeared. He began to experiment with a strange new power he termed 'Animal Magnetism,' which he claimed healed solely through magnetic force. Mesmer saw himself as a scientist, rather than a physician, for he believed he had discovered far more than a new method of treating disease. He saw it as a new physical force which he defined in his book, *Memoirs on the Discovery of Animal Magnetism.*

Mesmer taught his method to at least three hundred students, who then began to practice Animal Magnetism throughout Europe. His work met with great opposition from the medical profession. A commission was appointed by the King of France to investigate his claim to heal through magnetism. The report of the commission claimed that magnetism, without imagination on the subject's part, could produce no effect, and people were warned of the moral dangers involved. It was also noted that the effects of magnetism were directed and intensified by the will. The commission's report did little to dampen the popularity of Mesmer's work. Thus, he brought about the first recognition of mental causes as related to mental cures.

A student of Mesmer, Marquis de Puyse Gur, found that his own hypnotic work often produced a trance in his patient that put him into a deep sleep. Furthermore, he could control the patient, and even cure him, while he was in this trance. He concluded that the secret of Animal Magnetism was, in two words, *Belief* and *Will.* He wrote of the existence of a force by which the soul can work upon the body. "Animal Magnetism does not consist in the action of one body upon another, but in the action of the thought upon the vital principle of the body." His mesmerized subject, he learned, could hear no voice but his own, could feel no touch, and could obey no influence but his. The existence of an exclusive rapport between operator and subject, he concluded, was the surest test of the magnetic state. The subject would obey the slightest gesture, or even the silent will of the operator.

In the beginning, Mesmer and his students combined their hypnotic powers with various material props. By the early 1800's, these were discarded and the effort to trace hypnotism to mechanistic causes dropped away. Magnetism was explained as due to the imagination of the subject, alive to the least suggestion by word, look, gesture or even unexpressed thought from the operator. Furthermore, there was discovered that one in an induced trance would obey post-hypnotic suggestions, and an operator could hypnotize a subject from a distance.

Those pioneering in this work were usually seeking a means for relieving the suffering of mankind. Magnetism was promoted as an anesthetic until ether and chloroform were discovered.

Europe was the spawning ground of Mesmerism. It came to England and America from the Continent in the early part of the nineteenth century. Animal Magnetism was first effectively introduced into America in 1838. By the mid 1800's, it was called *mesmerism* or *hypnotism*, and there were a number of periodicals devoted exclusively to its theory and practice.

At this time, there entered a new phase of mesmerism. In some instances a subject, in a trance, seemed to make contact with those who had passed on. There were also those whose magnetic trances seemed to make them spiritual healers and 'inspirational speakers.' These events led to spiritualism. The magnetic trance seemed the door to the spiritual world, a touchstone with the dead, and a key to the mysteries of heaven.

In the latter part of the nineteenth century, mesmerism, spiritualism, and animal magnetism, declined in popularity. Scientific discoveries so clearly explained the universe as a material or mechanistic phenomena that spiritualism and magnetic healing were excluded from any classification as a science.

But with the physics of the twentieth century, all matter was reduced to waves of energy, and still the scientists did not find a final material cause for the universe. Instead, there came to light another dimension to creation — a non-material or mental dimension. This discovery has brought a renewed interest in all things mental — including hypnotism. As the power of hypnotism becomes generally known, many who understand it constantly warn against the evil use of it. The use of secret hypnotic work for evil ends is now widely recognized as a threat to individual freedom and well-being.

Hypnotism Defined

The resurgence of hypnotism has brought with it a sophisticated abuse of mental power that Mesmer and his followers neither understood nor practiced. The modern study of it has presented a more thorough understanding of its power and operation. *Hypnotism works through a person's susceptibility to mental suggestion, for it has been discovered that the human mind is very susceptible to suggestion.* Under the ethical use of hypnotism, the subject must consent to being hypnotized. He does not try to control his own mind, or resist the thoughts of the hypnotist. Through suggestions, the hypnotist puts the subject into a trance, and the hypnotist's commands come to replace the subject's own thoughts. The hypnotist's thoughts are the substance of the subject's thoughts, and the subject's emotional responses are in accordance with what the hypnotist suggests to him.

The subject may go into varying degrees of 'sleep' or trance. When a subject is in a deep hypnotic trance, the hypnotist is in complete control of him. The subject will hear and obey only the voice of the hypnotist. The subject will do what the operator tells him to do and experience what he suggests, including extreme pain, heroic experiences, and hallucinations. The operator can tell the subject that he will not remember being hypnotized, and the operator can plant post-hypnotic suggestions in the subject's mind that he must obey after the trance is broken. The operator can also program the subject so that he cannot be hypnotized by someone else. He can also cause hallucinations to continue after the trance.

It has been proven that a person may not be hypnotized if he is aware of the attempt, and does not give his consent. *However, he can be hypnotized without his consent if he is hypnotized without knowing he is being hypnotized!* It is possible for a hypnotist to secretly influence and control the unguarded mind.

The simple exhibitions of hypnotic control found in theaters and nightclubs, are child's play compared to the sophisticated and far-reaching practice of hypnosis that scientific studies have developed. The discovery that the human mind readily accepts hypnotic suggestion when it is unguarded, has implications that defy the imagination.

No one today seems safe from malicious mental attack. Outside of Christian Science, there apparently is no certain means known for counteracting this influence, and remaining in control of one's own mind.

This brief history of hypnotism is intended to show that in its origin and development, it in no way resembles spiritual healing found in Christian Science. Hypnotism relies on the will-power of the human mind, while spiritual healing is the action of the divine Mind on the human mind.

References:

Animal magnetism has no scientific foundation, for God governs all that is real, harmonious, and eternal, and His power is neither animal nor human. Its basis being belief and this belief animal, in Science animal magnetism, mesmerism, or hypnotism is a mere negation, possessing neither intelligence, power, nor reality, and in sense it is an unreal concept of the so-called mortal mind.

The mild forms of animal magnetism are disappearing, and its aggressive features are coming to the front. The looms of crime, hidden in the dark recesses of mortal thought, are every hour weaving webs more complicated and subtle. So secret are the present methods of animal magnetism that they ensnare the age into indolence, and produce the very apathy on the subject which the criminal desires. (S&H p 102)

Mary Baker Eddy's Exposure of Malpractice

In contrast to the dark origins of hypnotism, with its gradual development into modern-day mind control, Christian Science, with its healing power, has its roots in the Bible. It is a divine revelation that establishes the healing work of Christ Jesus on a scientific foundation.

Prior to her discovery of Christian Science, Mrs. Eddy had endured prolonged ill health. Along with her prayers for healing, she had investigated every kind of cure, including homeopathy and allopathy. In 1862, she went to Portland, Maine, for treatment with a famous mesmeric healer, Dr. Phineas Quimby. Quimby had a great talent for 'magnetic healing.' He was basically a good man who found he could relieve the suffering of others through hypnosis. He was not a religious man, but a humanitarian practitioner of hypnotic healing. He is said to have called God the 'Great Mesmerizer.'

Because Dr. Quimby was a magnetic healer, Mrs. Eddy found that the help she received from him was not permanent, nor did his work resemble spiritual healing as Mrs. Eddy later established it. In her search for an explanation of Christ Jesus' healing works, Mrs. Eddy at first mistook Quimby's magnetic healing for the second coming of the Christ.

Mrs. Eddy's tireless search for the scientific explanation

of Jesus' healing work, came to fruition in 1866 when she discovered Christian Science. Like the Master Christian, she "plunged beneath the material surface of things, and found the spiritual cause." Having discovered the scientific laws underlying his healing work, she then recorded the vision in her writings, especially *Science and Health with Key to the Scriptures*, known as the Christian Science textbook.

Early in her efforts to establish the Cause of Christian Science, her brief experience with Quimby proved invaluable, for it gave her first hand experience regarding the workings of mesmerism. She learned to separate spiritual healing from hypnotic cures, and open the eyes of her students to the difference. She also foresaw the great danger in the development of hypnotic power as a form of mind control.

In the nineteenth century, the world was innocent concerning malicious malpractice, and the harmful effects of hypnotism. Mrs. Eddy, herself, did not grasp the full implication of secret, malicious hypnotic work until several years after her discovery. Her first experience with it came from one of her students, Richard Kennedy. He seemed a promising healer, who began to take patients and do healing work under her coaching. When she found that he was mixing her teachings with the hypnotic practice of rubbing the heads of patients, she asked him to stop. Because of this and other differences between them, he became estranged from her, and then turned on her with a vengeance. He found that he could silently suggest to Mrs. Eddy's patients, whom she had healed, all the symptoms of a former illness, and the illness would return. He also began silently handling the thoughts of her students, suggesting that they turn on her, and leave her.

Mrs. Eddy was at first baffled by the reversal of her healing work, and her students' animosity and desertion, until she detected the silent hypnotic work of Kennedy. Her first edition of *Science and Health* warns against malpractice. The third edition has a chapter on 'Demonology' which was so strong that it frightened the readers. This chapter was soon reduced to twelve pages, for she found it best to leave unsaid much about malicious malpractice. She did teach promising students about malicious animal magnetism or M.A.M., as she called it. She also taught on mental assassination, mental poison and electrical poison, but she was hopelessly ahead of her time. Some of her students thought she was a fanatic on the subject of evil. Others were so frightened of it, that they wanted nothing more to do with Christian Science. But those who understood her teachings went on to become great pioneers in the Cause.

When Mrs. Eddy began the *Journal of Christian Science*, the early volumes had a section on 'Animal Magnetism,' carrying articles and experiences on handling malicious malpractice. She taught about the use of secret hypnotic work by the Jesuits and priests of the Roman Catholic Church. She warned against theosophy and witchcraft. Most important, *she taught how to resist and annul silent hypnotic attacks and protect the mind through scientific prayer.*

Mrs. Eddy recognized the power of malpractice to deaden the Christ-consciousness, to reverse spiritual healing, to substitute mortal thoughts for God's thoughts, and to obstruct the flow of spiritual inspiration that heals and regenerates. She revealed that the human mind is extremely susceptible to the influence of the mental atmosphere around it. She saw that the widespread use of hypnotism was inevitable. Her writings on it are as though they were written for today, and in her discovery of Christian Science, she gave us the ultimate means for overcoming all forms of hypnotism — *a metaphysical system of ideas that explains the allness of God and the unreality of evil, and the prayer of affirmation and denial.*

References:

The natural fruits of Christian Science Mind-healing are harmony, brotherly love, spiritual growth and activity. The malicious aim of perverted mind-power, or animal magnetism, is to paralyze good and give activity to evil. It starts factions and engenders envy and hatred, but as activity is by no means a right of evil and its emissaries, they ought not to be encouraged in it. Because this age is cursed with one rancorous and lurking foe to human weal, those who are the truest friends of mankind, and conscientious in their desire to do right and to live pure and Christian lives, should be more zealous to do good, more watchful and vigilant. Then they will be proportionately successful and bring out glorious results.

Unless one's eyes are opened to the modes of mental malpractice, working so subtly that we mistake its suggestions for the impulses of our own thought, the victim will allow himself to drift in the wrong direction without knowing it. Be ever on guard against this enemy. Watch your thoughts, and see whether they lead you to God and into harmony with His true followers. Guard and strengthen your own citadel more strongly. Thus you will grow wiser and better through every attack of your foe, and the Golden Rule will not rust for lack of use or be misinterpreted by the adverse influence of animal magnetism. (My p 213)

The more useful and prominent you become, the harder the mental robbers will work to rob you of good thoughts, a strong purpose and wise efforts to do God's will.
(DC p 49)

The higher one senses harmony, the more sensitive he is to discord; the same in music. (DC p 8)

Further information about Mrs. Eddy's experience with Kennedy is found in the third edition of *Science and Health*, wherein she exposes his malicious mental work in the chapter titled "Demonology." This chapter, along with other articles on animal magnetism and malpractice are found in the Bookmark Collection titled "Handling Malicious Animal Magnetism."

MENTAL MALPRACTICE

Spiritual Intuition vs Malicious Malpractice

This brief account of the history of hypnotism and Mrs. Eddy's encounter with it, is given to show that the two are entirely unrelated. An infinite gulf exists between scientific prayer and hypnotism. Through Christian Science, we learn the difference between the influence of malpractice controlling, damaging, even destroying the mind, and the influence of prayer healing, protecting and transforming it; the difference between spiritual healing and dominion, and hypnotic cures and mind control.

There is one element in human consciousness, however, that both animal magnetism and the divine Mind seem to share — *each has the ability to influence the human mind.* When the human mind is open to suggestion, the aggressive mental suggestions of animal magnetism can project negative, mortal beliefs into the mind, and so implant in it false beliefs that are imaged forth in every kind of discord. This transference of mortal thought from one mind to another takes place only within the *mortal realm of consciousness.* Malpractice brings loss of mental control, and alienates the mind from God.

However, we cannot afford to suppress this sensitivity to outside influence by becoming hard, cold, and insensitive, for this sensitivity is actually the means through which we communicate with God. Receptivity to the influence of divine Mind is the avenue through which God's thoughts unfold to us. The element of suggestibility that enables animal magnetism to reach us, is essentially the same element of receptivity through which God reaches us. However, thoughts from God bring peace, inspiration, enlightenment, understanding. They rescue the individual from evil; whereas the thoughts from animal magnetism bring loss of control, darkness, confusion, disturbance and deadens the inner rapport with God. The deeper one goes into Christian Science, the more sensitive he is to the influence of both.

18

Since we cannot block out our sensitivity to outside influence, we need to be knowledgeable about animal magnetism and malpractice, and we need to learn all we can about God.

As we turn a receptive mind to God and reach out to Him, we discover that God is very active in influencing the human mind. He is as close to us as our thoughts. In the heart of consciousness, angels — "God's thoughts passing to man" — appear as new ideas. At one time, these ideas are not known to us, and then they are. These revelations from God are the one true escape from every form of evil, for they spiritualize consciousness and fill it with divine Truth and Love. Thus, we are protected from malpractice, because mortal beliefs and spiritual ideas cannot both occupy the same mind at the same time. They are complete opposites. Therefore, the more we fill consciousness with spiritual thoughts, the more we are protected from hypnotic control. And so through daily study and prayer, we are learn to dwell in "the secret place of the most high."

With malpractice becoming so aggressive, subtle and secretive, it is imperative that we understand Mrs. Eddy's teaching on this subject. The time has come when those with spiritual understanding and moral integrity, must learn to defend themselves and others against the hypnotic influence of evil minds.

As spiritual understanding, gained from the study of Christian Science, arms us with divine intelligence, we can claim our dominion over the evil works of the malpractitioner. Thus, the age-old conflict between good and evil becomes a mental battle, and it will be in the purely mental realm that the final war between good and evil is fought, and the Christ triumphs over the antichrist.

Chapter III

AN ANALYSIS OF MALPRACTICE

Mrs. Eddy's deep concern over malpractice was surely due to her discernment of its inevitable threat to humanity, as the depraved mind of mortals learned to use it. Her published and unpublished writings on it indicate that there is far more to hypnotism than the use of it to entertain or relieve suffering. Since so little has been written on this subject in Christian Science, I am exploring it mainly through my own experience and statements found in Mrs. Eddy's writings. I have learned in Christian Science how to detect many subtle and undefined forms of malpractice and prevent them from influencing me. I share this experience to help you understand the challenges malpractice presents. The demonstration of Christian Science is so individual that no one can outline for another how to work out his own salvation. But I know that if I had been given some preliminary teachings on malpractice, it would have made my work much easier. My purpose in this discussion, is not to frighten you, but to so enlighten you that your lessons in malpractice will be easier than I found mine to be.

The Need to Handle Malpractice

In order to gain dominion over hypnotic influence, we must go much deeper into the subject than the general concept of it. The average person today may look upon hypnotism as mainly the act of one mind knowingly working to control another. Whether the hypnotist is working publicly to entertain an audience, or privately to cure a patient, or secretly to commit an invasion of another's mind for devious reasons, still the hypnotist knows how to exercise his mental powers over another mind.

Since we do not, as a rule, encounter hypnotists in the act of hypnotizing, we may be inclined to think there is no need to be concerned about malpractice. Because Christian Science teaches that God is All-in-all, and evil is unreal, some Scientists casually dismiss malpractice as nothing, and dwell only in absolute statements of truth. They believe that malpractice cannot affect them if they do not acknowledge it as a reality, or allow it to come into their experience. But such assumptions are extremely naive. Working only in the absolute is not enough to protect us from the harmful effects of many forms of malpractice.

In Christian Science, animal magnetism is exposed as nothing because an understanding of Science will destroy evil — actually reduce it to non-existence — proving it to be nothing but illusion. But we have this dominion over evil only when we can face every claim of animal magnetism, render it powerless, and destroy it through our metaphysical work. To turn away from a claim and say it is unreal, when to human sense it is very much a seeming reality — this is not handling it in Christian Science. In our metaphysical work, we must handle each claim and overcome it. *There are times when a claim will not yield until we handle malpractice.* Ignorance regarding malpractice leaves us undefended against it; yet we daily encounter hidden forms of it that can cause us untold discord, suffering, and pain.

For this reason, we need to examine the full range of malpractice as Mrs. Eddy taught her students to do. *She not only discerned the criminal and lethal use of hypnotism; she also had a much more expansive concept of thought transference, which included the constant exchange of negative thoughts and emotions that take place in our daily life.*

Reference:

Be strong and clear in your convictions that God, not M.A.M. [Malicious Animal Magentim], is influencing your actions. In order to be this, you surely must pray daily that God, good, divine Love — your only Mind — be followed, be loved, be lived by you. (DC p 128)

Malpractice the Cause of Problems

We need to be aware of all forms of malpractice for several reasons. First we are striving through prayer to meet every problem, or claim, that comes into our experience. If we do not have some insight into the workings of malicious animal magnetism, we eventually come upon claims that seem to defy our best effort to meet them. In such instances, malicious malpractice can contribute to the problem; it may even be the cause of it. If we do not understand malpractice, it can prevent healing, and obstruct our spiritual progress without our knowing what the real cause is, and how to handle it.

If a problem defies our own work and that of a more experienced Scientist, we may begin to doubt our work, another's work, and even Christian Science, unless we know how to determine if the claim is due to malpractice, and if so, how to treat it.

To be sure, a stubborn claim is usually due to false traits and beliefs in our own mortal thinking. So we cannot automatically attribute it to malpractice.

However, when a problem does not heal after a reasonable length of time, or it keeps recurring, we should know how to handle malpractice. In so doing, if in handling it, our work brings a change in the claim, then the cause is probably malpractice. Thus, the more knowledgeable we are concerning malpractice, the more effective our healing work.

There is a second reason for learning to handle malprac-

22

tice. Before we begin our work in Christian Science, our mind is easily influenced and handled by animal magnetism. But as we progress, we gain more and more dominion over our thinking. We spiritualize consciousness, until animal magnetism can no longer influence or control our thinking as easily as it did, and it begins to lose control over us. When it can no longer influence us from within, it will often attack us through the malpractice of others. Such malpractice usually comes through those closest to us. Our daily metaphysical work may chemicalize the atmosphere around us, and create conflict and discord seemingly for no reason. Unless we understand what is taking place, we may think we are failing in Christian Science, or blame ourselves for the discord, or become discouraged by problems that do not yield to our work.

Instead, we should recognize that our spiritual progress and success in Christian Science is causing animal magnetism to use others as an avenue through which to strike at us. At such times, we need to understand that it is not persons, but animal magnetism coming at us through outside sources because it can no longer control us from within. When we see this, we can rise above personal sense, look through and beyond the person, and recognize the real cause of the problem. If we impersonalize the attack and see the discord as evil trying to obstruct our spiritual progress, we can deal with it scientifically.

The sooner we learn to recognize the influence of malpractice, the easier our work in Science becomes. With each stage of progress, we usually encounter some form of malpractice. If we learn to handle it, we are constantly moving ever deeper into the spiritual realm, and establishing a wider gulf between ourselves and animal magnetism. Always remember that, whatever the trial, it only serves to lift us out of the belief of life in matter, and carry us further into divine reality. Through these spiritual lessons, we become increasingly sensitive to God's influence, while learning to rule out the fatal influence of animal magnetism.

Reference:

I (Mrs. Eddy) am meeting the serpent in its phases. There is not one belief of sickness that comes from my individuality. I now have to overcome that which says I feel other people's thought; that if it cannot touch you it will work through someone and reach you; this is the theosophical line of work. (DC p 16)

(7/16/05) Beloved Students at Pleasant View: Handle electricity of mortal mind; no arsenical poison, no belief of nerves. Love governs all. One Mind, one Truth. God is All-in-all. Jesus knew the hour of temptation and *wept*, but he also knew the power of Love supreme over all the errors of sense. No lie *stands* in the presence of Truth. No theosophy, black magic. No destructive electricity. "He commanded and it stood fast." God, good, is All. (DC p 54)

Malpractice Compared to Christian Science Treatment

We come now to a very basic key in understanding malpractice. I cannot emphasize enough the need to take this analysis to heart, and use it wisely.

We suffer from malpractice because the negative thoughts and emotions of another enter our consciousness, and we come under their influence. Their thoughts erroneously affect our thoughts. They seem to affect or control our mind and emotions, and prevent us from thinking and acting as we normally do. Consider this carefully: *malicious malpractice can be defined as a Christian Science treatment in reverse.*

A Christian Science treatment is the prayer of affirmation and denial. It affirms the truth about God and man, and denies the reality of evil and matter. An inspired treatment is a powerful form of divine intelligence that heals not only the person praying, but those upon whom his thoughts rest. When a Christian Science practitioner affirms the truth and denies a claim for a patient, his thoughts reach the patient's receptive mind and this mental work, filled with spiritual love and understanding, actually neutralizes and destroys the mesmerism of the claim. Healing takes place. This illustrates how the thinking of one mind can free another of the hypnotic influence of animal magnetism, and restore him to health. We see here how the influence for good in one mind can affect another. The practitioner's metaphysical work reaches the patient's consciousness, and brings about a better mental atmosphere, relieving pain and suffering, and bringing about healing.

Malpractice has exactly the opposite effect on the person to whom it is directed. It is the antitheses of a Christian Science treatment. When someone holds negative thoughts and emotions towards another, he malpractices on him, and his thoughts can cause the other person to suffer. He is in essence treating his victim with animal magnetism, rather than seeing him as a spiritual idea in God's likeness. Whenever mortal emotions inflame one's thoughts, and he allows himself to be handled by hatred, anger, animosity, self-justification, meanness, criticism, revenge, jealousy, envy, lust, etc., then these emotions move forth to inflict suffering, pain, and mental distress on the individual towards whom they are directed. *Such ungodlike thoughts are a negative treatment in which one affirms the error and denies the truth about another.* The malpractitioner argues emotionally for the error in another as he sees it, and in so doing, denies the victim's spiritual selfhood, and affirms, even intensifies, the mortal beliefs and emotions in the victim's mind. To direct such a personal vendetta against another makes a reality of discord and conflict, and afflicts another through anger and hatred. Such malpractice brings upon the victim mental and physical pain, distress, and anguish through the malpractitioner's hateful mental arguments. Such negative arguments are the antichrist of one mortal mind attacking the mentality of another, causing him to suffer for the duration of the attack.

Malicious malpractice affects another because of the *aggressive negative emotions* underlying it. When a malpractitioner is controlled by the emotions of animal magnetism, he does not need to be trained in hypnotism in order to harm another. Malpractice coming from the hatred of the carnal mind can inflict mental and physical suffering upon others by the sheer aggressiveness and intensity of its hatred, or its desire to control, dominate, manipulate, or see another suffer.

Revenge, bitterness, unforgiveness, criticism, the entire range of mortal emotions — when focused on another — can have a devastating effect on his health and well-being. Such emotional vendetta directed towards the unsuspecting mind, is a treatment in reverse. It can have a harmful effect on him long after the attack is over.

For this reason, it is essential in Christian Science to understand why we cannot hold unloving thoughts of another, and why we must at the same time be able to detect and defend ourselves against the negative thoughts and emotions of both the ignorant and malicious malpractitioner.

Reference:

The mental stages of crimes, which seem to belong to the latter days, are strictly classified in metaphysics as some of the many features and forms of what is properly denominated, in extreme cases, moral idiocy. . . .

This mental disease at first shows itself in extreme sensitiveness; then, in a loss of self-knowledge and of self-condemnation, — a shocking inability to see one's own faults, but an exaggerating sense of other people's. Unless this mental condition be overcome, it ends in a total loss of moral, intellectual, and spiritual discernment, and is characterized in this Scripture: "The fool hath said in his heart, There is no God." This state of mind is the exemplification of total depravity, and the result of sensuous mind in matter. Mind that is God is not in matter; and God's presence gives spiritual light, wherein is no darkness. . . .

Whoever is mentally manipulating human mind, and is not gaining a higher sense of Truth by it, is losing in the scale of moral and spiritual being, and may be carried to the depths of perdition by his own consent. He who refuses to be influenced by any but the divine Mind, commits his way to God, and rises superior to suggestions from an evil source. Christian Science shows that there is a way to escape from the latter-day ultimatum of evil, through scientific truth; and so all are without excuse. (Mis p 112)

Conscious obedience to the open or secret demands of evil minds, ensures moral and physical death. Ignorant submission to these evil though inaudible demands is sure doom. Your eyes must be opened, that you may see and feel this hidden influence; for if you only understood its cause you would besiege it with Science, until you compelled the city of evil to capitulate, and so saved yourself. Science is more exacting than sense; it abates not one demand. All possible progress in Christian Science is sacrificed by him who yields to the influence of animal magnetism. Knowing this, the envious mental malpractitioner, intent on reducing you to his standard, sends to you, mentally, his demoralizing arguments; but at the same moment he whispers into your thought: "I am not influencing you; it is such and such a one." (DC p 148)

The only power there is in mesmerism is what we allow it to have. . . . Truth reflects itself and what the Principle does its idea also does. So error tries to accomplish a certain result and its idea does the same thing! One mortal mind cannot touch another. Their thoughts meet each other part way. One never comes up to the other; that is but the belief. (DC p 178)

Evil thoughts and aims reach no farther and do no more harm than one's belief permits. Evil thoughts, lusts, and malicious purposes cannot go forth, like wandering pollen, from one human mind to another, finding unsuspecting lodgement, if virture and truth build a strong defence. (S&H p 234)

There is nothing about me that attracts, corresponds with, or responds to, any form of error or evil. In proportion to your realization of this are you immune to the mesmeric and hypnotic influences of A.M. [animal magnetism]. (DC p 79)

Never fear a lie. Declare against it with the conviction of its nothingness. Throw your whole weight into the right scale — this is the way to destroy evil. Never weigh against yourselves by admitting a lie. (DC p 175)

Malpractice and Mortal Emotions

The force underlying malpractice comes from the *emotional* basis of the mortal disposition. Malpractice is driven more by mortal feelings, than reason and intellect. It is not what one thinks, but what he feels, that causes others to suffer. It is his personal emotions that renders malicious malpractice so harmful.

The human disposition includes fear, self-will, and hatred in varying degrees. The more void one is of the Christ-consciousness, the deeper he is submerged in animal magnetism, and so the stronger the mortal emotions, the more aggressive and threatening the malpractice when these emotions surface! *The hateful, angry, willful thoughts one holds towards another are the driving energy behind the mental and physical pain inflicted by malpractice.* When we are controlled by mortal emotions, we tend to malpractice on others, and in so doing, we suffer from this mental disobedience to God's laws, and we cause them to suffer.

Mortal emotions are the common ground through which the mind both influences and is influenced by malpractice. The false traits in our own mortal disposition — anger, hurt, fear, self-will, self-justification, revenge, jealousy, hate — all of these elements within consciousness cause us to malpractice on others. They also lead to mutual malpractice, or an exchange of aggressive mental suggestion that harms both parties. While human opinion, rationalization, intellect and logic are part of the tendency to malpractice, it is mortal emotions that inflict the most pain and distress on another.

Mortal emotions in our own disposition also make us the victims of malpractice. As we learn about malpractice, we may tend to blame our problems on the malpractice of others; but in the last analysis, we are responsible for our own state of mind. *If we appear to be suffering from the thoughts of others, it is because consciously or unconsciously, we have allowed their malpractice to enter our mental atmosphere through our own mortal beliefs and emotions.*

There must be some consent within our own consciousness through which another's thoughts can reach us. The fear of malpractice itself will be an opening for aggressive hypnotic influence. Our own basic mortal nature, our own self-will, hatred and fear are in agreement with the minds around us. These emotions are the avenues through which malpractice handles us. Even a simple, seemingly justified emotion can be the opening for malpractice — such as feeling responsible for another, wanting good for him, being concerned for him, being dependent upon him, fearing him, and so on. Through even seemingly normal personal attachment, the thoughts of another can adversely affect us, for malpractice takes place in personal sense.

As our understanding of Christian Science and malpractice increases, we find *there is always some mortal element within our own thinking that lets in the thoughts of others. There is no exception to this.* We are in some way receptive to the aggressive mental suggestions that affect us.

This fact gives us the promise of total protection from malpractice. As we spiritualize consciousness, we eliminate the mortal elements that allow the thoughts and emotions of others to influence us. Through divine intelligence, we can foresee and forestall the intrusion of harmful hypnotic suggestion, and then we cannot be made to suffer from the ungodlike thoughts of others.

The Effects of Malpractice

Malpractice is a subtle influence that very often catches us undefended. Therefore we should be aware of the many different ways it claims to affect us mentally, emotionally and physically. It would be logical to assume that if we are meeting malicious malpractice, we ourselves would express a similar hatred or anger. And, in fact, we may find ourselves feeling angry towards another involuntarily. Hatred or anger directed towards us can seem to bring about an unnatural angry, defensive reaction on our part. We may mentally rehearse a conflict to ourselves, argue, justify, and explain our words or actions over and over again to our opponent, and continue doing so long after we want to forget the entire thing. Such lack of mental control indicates that the other person is attacking us mentally with a great deal of hostility and anger. His thoughts and emotions, like a negative treatment, are entering our consciousness, and mesmerizing us into a mental argument or reply to his accusations.

Here we have one of the most common indications of malpractice. When we find we cannot stop thinking about an individual, mentally conversing with him, reasoning with him, arguing with him, etc., then he most likely is carrying on an angry vendetta against us. If someone is constantly on our mind without our wanting this, and we seem almost obsessed with thinking of him, this would indicate that we are meeting his malpractice.

But this reaction is not the only effect that malpractice has. The hatred of another can produce a wide range of reactions that are foreign to our normal disposition, and that we do not necessarily attribute to malpractice.

Malpractice can cause mental numbness; an inability to think clearly; abnormal fatigue; extreme nervousness or excitement; great fear, guilt and self-condemnation; deep depression and an overwhelming sense of futility; a mental darkness as though being totally separated from God; heaviness; a drug-like tendency to sleep during the day; sleepless nights; confusion and indecision; mental and physical pain. Malicious malpractice can come as the suggestion of a disease or physical disorder; the suggestion will persist until we believe and fear it, and this fear will cause the disease to appear on the body. Malicious malpractice can cause insanity, mental derangement, suicide and many kinds of seemingly incurable diseases and malfunctions. It can cause waves of terror to grip one. It can bring on the constant fear of accidents, disasters, things going wrong.

Many physical claims can be the result of malpractice — flu, colds, problems with teeth and gums, skin rashes, violent headaches, heart trouble, attacks of gas. Quite often a claim caused by malpractice simply "comes over us" without warning. There does not seem to be a reason for it. We have not been through any emotional experience that would explain why it comes, and why it also leaves.

Physical problems that repeatedly come and go, are usually due to malpractice. A physical illness or mental disturbance will suddenly come on one and then lift completely only to return again as before; or we will have one claim after another to meet, each as aggressive as the last one. A physical claim may seem to take different forms and move about the body, rather than remain one specific claim in one part of the body. Malpractice can also cause a return of old claims, or a reversal of a recent healing.

This list is given to indicate some of the many claims that can be due to malpractice. Those inexperienced in malpractice usually attribute its effects to other causes such as heredity, germs, age, even the tendency to 'have a bad day,' or to be moody or difficult. Treating claims caused by malpractice as being due to other causes may temporarily relieve the problem. But if we stop working, believing all is well, the effects of malpractice will return, and the same problem or another just as serious will come on us.

MENTAL MALPRACTICE

Many types of mental malpractice are so common that they take place around us daily. The average mind experiences malpractice as a normal part life. A quarrel or conflict, a fight or a heated difference of opinion, stirs up strong negative emotions, and these become malicious malpractice. Hostile thoughts affect one towards whom they are directed, whether the emotions are outwardly expressed or not. One possessed with hostility constantly malpractices. Once a confrontation takes place, those involved cannot assume that it is over when they part company. One or both usually will continue to harbor malicious thoughts towards the other, rehashing the conflict, arguing mentally with the other person, and feeling justified in his hatred towards his opponent. This malpractice, like a negative treatment, can inflict on the other person depression, mental darkness, disturbed emotions, extreme nervousness or weariness, or even a physical problem. By constantly arguing silently, hatefully, maliciously at the other person, the malpractitioner prevents him from thinking clearly and correctly for himself.

Many conscientious people who ignorantly malpractice on others, would never do so if they knew the suffering and pain it causes the victim. It takes a depraved mind to intentionally malpractice. Much of the mental malpractice that goes on in our day-to-day experience is ignorant, but the pain and suffering from it can be as devastating as the mental work of a trained hypnotist, when the emotions underlying it are extremely intense, personal, and hateful. Such malicious malpractice can take place with family, friends, neighbors, business or social contacts — wherever there is occasion for conflict. Mrs. Eddy once said, "Deny all kinds of mental poison. Mental poison is the mental atmosphere of conflicting human opinions and beliefs. We must handle the serpent and know its arguments are false and powerless since Mind alone is real." (*Divinity Course and General Collectanea*)

Reference: An excellent source of short, powerful treatments for handling animal magnetism and malpractice is found in *Watches, Prayers, Arguments*. This collection of treatments was given by Mrs. Eddy to the mental workers at Pleasant View. First published by Gilbert C. Carpenter, Jr., this collection is available as a complete transcript of the original book. However, a majority of these treatments can also be found in *Divinity Course and General Collectanea*. Both are available from The Bookmark.

Uncovering Malpractice as the Cause of Problems

It is often necessary to uncover the source of malpractice if one seems unable to meet the attack. An emotional estrangement, a misunderstanding, a heated argument — any experience which has brought about anger, hurt, unforgiveness, or animosity on the part of one or both parties — can result in suffering and pain to the one upon whom these negative emotions are directed. Quite often a claim will begin to give out when we detect the source of the malpractice, and vehemently and persistently deny the power of aggressive mental suggestion to affect us in any way.

Without Christian Science, it is difficult to determine whether or not one is being hypnotically influenced, because his mental atmosphere is so similar to those with whom he associates that there is little or no distinct contrast between his own thoughts and those being mentally suggested to him. Those who are buried in mortal mind are constantly malpracticing on each other, and then attributing the resulting illness and discord to material causes. They exchange hate, criticism, mortal beliefs of every kind, and they suffer from it accordingly. Therefore an understanding of malpractice not only helps us demonstrate Christian Science, but enables us to discern malpractice operating in the lives of others.

Malpractice is sometimes difficult to detect because it will appear as your own thoughts, but you become increasingly adept at

MENTAL MALPRACTICE

detecting the intrusion as you go ever deeper into Christian Science, for this Science lifts consciousness above the atmosphere of mortal mind. Then when antichrist thoughts try to reach you, the contrast between your normal state of mind and the aggressive mental suggestions is so great that you refuse to think them. Thus you "stand porter at the door of thought."

Chapter IV

PERSONAL MALPRACTICE

The subject of malpractice takes on a new dimension in Christian Science when we learn to detect its influence in our own personal relationships. Aggressive mental suggestions come from many unsuspected sources. We need to bring into focus the many types of malpractice that take place in the normal course of our daily life, in order to handle them scientifically.

By giving some examples of personal malpractice, I hope to open up to you an initial insight into the many ways in which hypnotic influence handles the undefended mind. This discussion does not cover all forms of personal malpractice. It is intended to help you undertake your own analysis of it.

Three Types of Malpractice

In *Miscellaneous Writings*, Mrs. Eddy states: "All mesmerism is one of three kinds; namely, the ignorant, the fraudulent, or the malicious workings of error or mortal mind."

Ignorant malpractice occurs when the negative thoughts and emotions of one person adversely influence another, even though the person has no intention of actually harming him. Personal negative emotions can cause another person varying degrees of mental distress and physical pain. Although ignorant malpractice is not a premeditated form of hypnotic control, it can cause another intense and prolonged suffering if the emotions underlying it are hateful, vindictive, angry, hard, bitter, unforgiving, malicious, etc.

Fraudulent malpractice is manipulation and control motivated by dishonesty. It is deceitful, cunning, calculating. It is always robbing and cheating others. The end result of fraudulent malpractice is always to the good of the malpractitioner and to the detriment of the victim. In the premeditated act of deceiving, robbing, and using another, a fraudulent malpractitioner may use secret hypnotic suggestion. Also the use of subliminal suggestion comes under this classification. Whenever we have been deceived by false advertising; or conned into buying something we do not really want, or doing something we do not want to do, or manipulated or deceived in any way, we have been the victim of fraudulent malpractice.

Malicious malpractice can be defined in two ways. First, there is the intentional use of hypnosis to control another. A trained hypnotist can use his mental powers to attack, and even destroy, another. His hypnotic work can be lethal, and he has no reluctance to use it in achieving his goal. Malicious malpractice is the ultimate mind control, and outside of Christian Science, there is nothing to protect the mind from the attack of a malicious mind that who knows how to use its mental powers to control or destroy others.

Second, there are times when ignorant or fraudulent malpractice is malicious. Even though the malpractitioner knows nothing about hypnosis, the malice motivating his words and deeds can be as destructive as that of a trained hypnotist.

A distinct line cannot always be drawn between these three types of malpractice. Fraudulent and ignorant malpractice can be malicious, and malicious malpractice can be ignorant. Much depends on the source of the malpractice. Not only are we at times the victims of malpractice, but we unknowingly malpractice on ourselves and others far more than we realize.

In order to explain how much malpractice appears to operate in our daily life, we can classify malpractice in the following categories:

1. *Self Malpractice*
2. *Personal Malpractice*
3. *Collective Malpractice*
4. *Scientific and Medical Malpractice*
5. *Secret Occult Malpractice*

We should have some insight into these various forms of malpractice, but we must also take care not to make malpractice so real that we begin to fear it. While we cannot ignore malpractice, neither should we fear it, or become obsessed with it. It is the purpose of this discussion to present a general knowledge of it which will help you detect and handle it in Christian Science.

Self Malpractice

The most harmful malpractice we encounter comes from our own mind. We malpractice on ourselves when we turn our negative thoughts and emotions inward to our own shortcomings and limitations. *In fact, it is more harmful to think one negative thought about yourself than for ten people to think it about you.*

The most devastating malpractice we encounter, is that in which we disapprove of ourselves; criticize and dislike ourselves; feel inadequate, guilty and self-condemning; indulge in self-recrimination; argue that we are unloved, unwanted, and shut out of all good, etc. Every negative thought we hold towards ourselves is a form of malpractice that tends to cloud over our spiritual selfhood in God's likeness. We mesmerize ourselves into believing negative, limiting, harmful claims about ourselves, and we suffer accordingly.

Stop and consider how many times each day you could be malpracticing on yourself by thinking, I can't possibly do that; I'm getting old; I'm tired; I'm going to catch the flu; I have a bad habit of always being late. Day in and day out, we project the very things we don't want to experience into our life by thinking erroneously about ourselves. This subtle form of malpractice needs long and serious consideration. As we study Christian Science, we learn of man made in God's image; then we must meet the demand to reflect this image. To do this, we must stop influencing our own mind to think negative thoughts of ourselves. As we work to know God and man in His image, spiritual understanding replaces the false image of man with the true one, and we no longer malpractice on ourselves.

Through daily metaphysical work, we learn to discipline our thinking to think in spiritual ideas. We gain control of our mind. If we have no experience in disciplining thought, the mind wanders over endless mental terrain. We involuntarily recall bad relationships, rehash bad experiences, converse or argue with another, justify or explain ourselves to everyone, and go from thing to thing to thing with no direction or focus. We may rehearse disturbing experiences over and over. Lack of mental discipline prevents us from focusing on any one thing for more than a few seconds.

This inability to control our mind is malpractice taking place internally, for it is mortal mind we are rehearsing. When we do this, we are an easy target for aggressive mental suggestions, since we are already in a negative mode of thought. Being on the same plane of thought as most of the world, we cannot tell when we are being hypnotically influenced. We don't know if we are thinking our thoughts or the thoughts of another.

Moreover, as we malpractice on ourselves, we ignorantly malpractice on others, for we are entertaining negative thoughts and emotions about them as well. Just as their wrong thinking affects us, our wrong thinking affects them. Malpractice is a two-way street.

As we study Christian Science, and stop thinking negative

38

thoughts about ourselves and others, we lift thought above mortal mind, into a spiritual atmosphere filled with God's thoughts. Being receptive to God's thoughts, we are protected from the thoughts of mortal mind. It is a great achievement to take control of your mind, and so govern your thoughts and emotions that malpractice cannot enter it. From this we see that real protection from hypnotic control begins when we stop malpracticing on ourselves, and learn to discipline the mind to think in spiritual ideas, rather than the illusions of mortal mind.

Malpractice in Personal Relationships

Closely related to self-malpractice, is the ignorant malpractice that takes place in personal relationships through the daily one-on-one exchange of mortal thoughts and feelings. Ignorant malpractice comes through our contact with family, relatives and friends, business, social and associates, casual acquaintances, wherever mind meets mind. When we exchange fearful, negative, disturbing, mental impressions of any kind, when we rehearse error to another, we ignorantly malpractice, for the negative thoughts we share in our relationships, transfers animal magnetism from one mind to another.

Consider how much each day you talk about your own discordant relationships and experiences, sickness, accidents, aggravations and difficulties, past and present; how you relay to others your disturbed, angry, disappointed, or fearful thoughts and emotions towards someone or something. And how much each day you take in a similar mortal picture conveyed to you by those you know.

How much do you engage in gossip — probably the most common form of ignorant malpractice? What happens when gossip goes from mind to mind to mind? When we rehearse the personal business of another, and then criticize and judge him, we are malpracticing. It is not really our intention to malpractice others, nor do they intend to malpractice us. Ignorant malpractice is a common occurrence; and in some relationships, it is a continuous onslaught of mortal mind to the smallest detail. Through this constant rehearsal of animal magnetism, this exchange of personal trials and tribulations, we malpractice on others, and they malpractice on us. Such malpractice serves to intensify and enlarge upon the very mortal mentality we are trying to overcome. We cannot study Christian Science for a few hours each day, and then spend the rest of the time sharing mortal thoughts and emotions with others, and then hope to gain our freedom from animal magnetism.

There are times, of course, when we must be in the company of those who rehearse error, and we may have to listen to it, but we are not obligated to rehearse our problems to them. Should we tell them of a claim we are having to meet, they will often attach it to us long after we have overcome it, and refuse to believe that the claim has been met.

You may find that as you close your mind to listening to mortal mind talk, less and less comes into your experience. You do not have to listen to one who talks incessantly, and insists that you listen to him while he imposes upon you an unending stream of mesmeric mortal mind talk. If the compulsive talker must tell you his experiences, problems, and beliefs, his voice temporarily replaces God's voice in consciousness. Such ignorant malpractice is a form of mental static that clogs the mind and separates you from God. Constant mortal mind talk is like another voice in consciousness demanding your attention, forcing you to focus your mind on mortal beliefs and opinions, personal sense testimony, conflicts and discord, animal magnetism in all its many forms. When you are constantly in the company of a compulsive talker, all spiritual progress stagnates until you can take control of things, and put a stop to it.

Much of the animal magnetism that we encounter during the day is ignorant malpractice. Yet to the extent that we take it in, it darkens the mind and clouds over our receptivity to God's thoughts. What greater loss is there than to lose the ability to hear God's voice because the mind is filled with claims of animal magnetism that have been transferred to our mind by ignorant malpractice?

Personal Sexual Malpractice

Because sexuality is considered a thing to be desired, aggressive sexual suggestion is seldom seen as malpractice. Yet one of the most disturbing forms of ignorant malpractice is that of sensualism. When one is lusting for another, this is sexual malpractice. Sexual malpractice can suggest to its victim abnormal sexual desire. Some individuals are far more sexual than others. The extremely sexual person may be attracted to the pure thought of a spiritually-minded person. This sexual desire then becomes a form of malpractice that reaches the object of desire through lust. When the malpractitioner is lusting after someone, his sexual desire will influence the other person sexually. Unless the victim understands such malpractice, he will not know that the sexual feelings that overcome him are from the hypnotic sexual influence of the malpractitioner.

Often when animal magnetism cannot handle a consecrated student of Christian Science in any other way, it will attack him or her through sensualism. The lust and passion handling a malpractitioner given to excessive sexual desires, is a form of malpractice that mesmerizes the subject of his sexual desire into acts of immorality. Such sexual desire may seem to be the victim's own feelings, whereas it is actually aggressive mental suggestion handling the undefended mind. Such malpractice can destroy a marriage, home, and family, and lead to financial and personal ruin. Because sensual malpractice makes the victim feel desirable and wanted, he or she may even believe the attraction is a demonstration. But a true demonstration leads out of mortal discord, out of the control of sexuality, into spiritual love, freedom and purity.

Today, with sexuality so blatantly exploited by the media, the student of Christian Science needs to be especially alert to the ignorant malpractice of another whose lust leads the student to mistake it for a genuine relationship based on mutual love, respect and true values. Sexual malpractice can be a serious threat to a student, and should be guarded against constantly. We can do much prayerful work to understand what sexual malpractice is, and how to handle it. Once we understand this, we cannot be drawn into a relationship we do not want, and should not have — one that will obstruct our spiritual progress, and pull us ever deeper into mental darkness.

Personal Fraudulent Malpractice

Malpractice motivated by deceit and dishonesty, is a constant threat today, for dishonesty can be extremely polished, sophisticated, subtle, cunning, clever, and convincing.

In our personal experience, we are exposed to salesmen talking us into something we don't want, advertising hype misrepresenting a product or service, a mechanic that promises a complete job and does as little as possible, an employee who won't work, and an employer who demands more work than he is willing to pay for. The area for marginal fraud has grown in proportion to the prosperity of our world.

From well disguised confidence games that offer vast returns for little or no investment, to the con artist who will take a retired bookkeeper's life savings — all of these are examples of fraudulent malpractice that can take place in our personal life.

Added to many age-old methods of fraud, we are now being influenced by psychological salesmanship, subliminal suggestion, and the actual use of hypnotism in sales.

Fraudulent malpractice is malicious malpractice, and can bring great suffering to the victim. The possibilities of being handled by fraudulent malpractice are so numerous that it takes more than good common sense to be protected from all fraud. Again, we find refuge in Christian Science. As we come to trust God to deliver us from all evil, our spiritual intuitions will tell us when we are being victimized by fraudulent malpractice, and how to prevent it from happening.

Personal Malicious Malpractice

Malicious malpractice is not confined to the work of trained hypnotists aggressively hypnotizing their victim. There are forms of malicious malpractice that take place in many personal relationships. We tend to think of such relationships as difficult, when actually they manifestations of malpractice. Examples can run the range from a controlling parent fearful for his or her child, to child abuse, battered wives, the hard-nosed businessman, and the 'little dictator.'

Malicious malpractice is found in the domineering, self-righteous, aggressive, self-willed person, who constantly manipulates or forces others to yield to his or her demands. He will not be crossed or defied. He insists on directing, managing, and controlling others. He often abuses without conscience.

Here we have one of the most important forms of malpractice to detect and handle, because it does not necessarily appear to be malicious malpractice, but simply a difficult, or impossible, relationship.

Malicious personal malpractice is the ultimate example of a treatment in reverse. It draws its seeming power from the emotions motivating it. One who is driven by selfishness and hatred, thinks and acts aggressively and maliciously. Such malice will hate, attack, argue, dominate and poison the mind and body of anyone who must endure a personal relationship with him. It is so harmful because the malpractitioner acts out of complete self-righteousness and self-justification in taking the action he does.

This mental state of unrelenting hostility, is one of the most destructive forms of malpractice that we ever encounter. It can come through one's family, relatives, friends, co-workers, church members. It is usually openly expressed in the critical, arguing, contradicting and condescending attitude with which the malpractitioner treats others. But his unspoken thoughts filled with hatefulness and depraved will, can inflict on his victim an unrelieved disturbed state of mind, in which the victim is constantly and silently answering, defending, arguing with, or trying to make peace with the malpractitioner. The constant effort to find ways of dealing with such a person, is enough to postpone indefinitely our progress in Christian Science.

Here we see how animal magnetism, coming at a student through another, claims to hold him in his present mortal state of mind, for he must constantly deal with one who is contentious, difficult, and generally a very 'thorny' person to be around. Such a relationship puts the victim under relentless malpractice. It attacks him daily, and in doing so, prevents him from concentrating on the study and prayerful work necessary to dissolve the relationship. When the malpractitioner is in the position daily to criticize and condemn his victim silently or openly, this unrelieved aggressive mental suggestion acts like a mental poison which can eventually kill the victim spiritually, mentally, physically. To be the object of another's depraved will and hatred can produce mental illness and physical disease that appear incurable.

Personal malicious malpractice is especially difficult to deal with because a malpractitioner will gather others into his camp, and cause them to join him in malpracticing on the victim. When one is in the constant company of two or more who have a hostile attitude towards him, this collective malpractice can be enough to bring about a mental and physical breakdown.

Malicious malpractice in our personal relationships is something that should be taken very seriously, for it is usually the source of many of our mental and physical problems. It may even be inflicted on us in the name of love and caring. If we do not know how to meet it in Christian Science, this daily dose of negative emotions will slowly poison the mind and body and lead to seemingly incurable and even fatal disease.

Too often, a victim will spend years enduring mental abuse, cruelty, and physical problems resulting from malicious malpractice. Since the disposition of the malpractitioner seems so hardened in mental traits that make him so malicious, there is little chance that he will change, and the victim's only hope of release from mental abuse, is to sever the relationship. Insanity and mental breakdown can be the end result of such prolonged malicious mental abuse, unless one is delivered from such a relationship.

I once knew a woman, a patient of mine, whose husband was one of the most domineering men I have ever met. Year after year he vented constant mental abuse on his family. To see this man with his wife in public, you would think it was a compatible marriage; but at home the husband was irrational and demanding, throwing temper tantrums over little or nothing. When he wasn't abusing his family, he was indifferent to them. His wife was a devoted student of Christian Science, but he would have nothing to do with it. She hoped and prayed for change in him, for she loved her family deeply; but as the years passed, the husband's disposition only grew worse.

From the early years of the marriage, the wife had many mental and physical problems which she had difficulty meeting in Christian Science. She would often awaken in the morning with a dark hopeless feeling which she would try to rise above during the day. She had spells of black depression, and was abnormally tired. She had severe attacks of flu and colds. It seemed as though she would hardly work out one problem before she had another to meet. All of these, she treated as claims coming from her own wrong thinking, and she did profit greatly from this effort to spiritualize her thoughts. However, as she progressed in Christian Science, she began to realize that many of her mental and physical problems were the direct result of the unrelieved malicious malpractice vented on her day in and day out by her husband. She began to have many serious physical problems, such as extreme attacks of gas, symptoms of a heart condition, and the most serious claim — an intense unrelieved pain in her head that would come on early in the morning and last all day, pain so severe she could hardly think. The relationships in the home were causing her constant stress and anxiety. She was nervous, tense, insecure, because of the uncertainty concerning her husband's behavior. Even when he showed no open attack of hatred, the malice towards his family was always present, destroying the peace and harmony of the home.

Finally, the pain in her head was so frequent and so severe that she felt that she was losing control of her mind. It was at this point that she managed to leave him, for she felt that she would not live much longer, if she continued to meet so much malice.

Within weeks after she left, all of the physical claims vanished. It was as though she had never had them. Had they been caused by her own thinking, they would have remained after she left; but instead, they completely disappeared.

During the years that she was experiencing this mental abuse, she worked constantly in Science to overcome the mortal traits in her own thinking that brought this relationship into her experience. As many false traits were overcome and replaced with spiritual qualities, she demonstrated her way out of the relationship. When she was finally free, she never again found herself permanently involved with a person of this nature.

I could give many examples of similar experiences where the person's mental and physical suffering was due to malpractice, but I use this one because it is so explicit in showing the relationship between malicious malpractice and the physical problems of the victim. In relationships where the victim has not been so fortunate as to be able to leave, he or she has passed on from such unrelieved mental abuse. Unrelenting malice and domination in a prolonged relationship, is one of the most common forms of personal malpractice resulting in extreme physical problems that defy healing in Christian Science.

It is important that we have insight into personal malicious malpractice, for it can take place in our own life and in the lives of those around us. When one or both parties in a relationship, have a disposition that is basically hateful, selfish, and willful, we have malicious malpractice. This hypnotic influence is motivated by the depraved emotions of animal magnetism; and it can be as lethal as that of a trained hypnotist, because the unrelieved presence of spoken and unspoken malice in a relationship wears down the victim's mental energies, and eventually can prove fatal.

However, these very experiences can be a blessing in disguise, for they force us deeper into Christian Science, and teach us to recognize when malicious malpractice is taking place in our own lives, and in the lives of others. They help us to free ourselves of such mental cruelty, and to understand the behavior of others who are involved in such discordant relationships.

Collective Malpractice

Most personal malpractice is a one-on-one experience. We give and/or receive aggressive mental suggestions that erroneously influence the mind. This could be called simple malpractice, in that the negative thoughts and emotions directed towards us are not, as a rule, so strong, aggressive, and unrelenting that we cannot counter-

act them in Christian Science. Unless we are involved in a relationship in which the malpractice is unrelieved malice, the effects
of malpractice should not be permanently crippling. Most encoun-
ters affect us temporarily. You may find that there are times when
the effects of malpractice lift as soon as the malpractice stops. As
a student grows increasingly astute in detecting malpractice, he
can almost sense to the minute when it has stopped, and when it
begins again. This helps to get through a challenging bout with it,
especially when one's metaphysical work is not enough to lift him
entirely above it. There are times when we may be unable to meet
a particularly malicious attack; but when we know what it is, we
can tough it out until the malpractitioner grows weary and gives up.

Collective malpractice is more difficult to counteract, in
that it is a more intensified and aggressive form of hypnotic influence. One type of collective malpractice comes about when two
or more minds together generate negative thoughts and feelings
about the same person. The negative influence of several minds
ignorantly, maliciously malpracticing on a mutual acquaintance,
friend, or member of the family, can have a serious and long-lasting
effect on the individual being attacked. The more minds involved,
the more disturbing and harmful the hypnotic attack. A victim may
be so deeply affected by the intensity of the malpractice that he is
months recovering. If the collective criticism, disapproval, hostility,
etc., is prolonged and extremely cruel, he may not be able to free
his mind of it for many years.

Examples of Collective Malicious Malpractice

The best example we have of collective malicious malpractice and its the lasting effects, is that which takes place in a
family. When several members of a family have a critical, disapproving, even hostile, attitude towards one member, this can be so
devastating that the individual never seems to recover from it. Many
abused children and young adults are permanently scarred by mali-

cious mental malpractice that they cannot erase from memory. These scars are forms of hypnotism so forcefully ingrained in consciousness that the victim cannot free his mind of them through any human means, and so they remain to affect him throughout his lifetime. These mental scars are aggressive mental suggestions that have become forms of self-malpractice. The hypnotic state has become so deeply entrenched in consciousness that, long after the relationships have terminated, the guilt, fear, self-condemnation, etc., brought on by the malpractice, remain. Such emotions are not part of his normal disposition, but a reaction to continuous exposure from an early age to malicious malpractice by the family.

Another common form of collective malpractice is gossip — ignorant, fraudulent and/or malicious gossip. To single out one person and spread personal gossip — hateful, disapproving, judgmental, snide, slanderous remarks and assumptions about him — from mind to mind to mind, is a form of malpractice that can demoralize and even destroy another. It is a concentrated form of hatred that has long-lasting effects. There is no way of measuring the harmful effects of collective gossip on an individual. When two or more minds focus in a negative way on one individual, they can create all kinds of mental and physical problems for him. The more minds involved and the more vicious the gossip, the more damaging the effect. The disapproval and criticism of relatives, church members, club members or those with whom one works, the gossip that goes from person to person to person, can build to such an intensity as to cause a mental and physical breakdown in the victim.

Public figures — the rich and the famous — have an overwhelming amount of collective malpractice to meet. The jealousy, envy, adoration, lust, emulation, and criticism that they meet from the public, can explain many of the unusual things they say and do. Such collective malpractice, coupled with the pressure to perform brilliantly, or maintain a public image, can cause the person under attack such mental and physical pain as to drive him to drink or drugs for relief.

At the other end of the scale, those who live in dark, depressing slums, may have to endure such intense or concentrated animal magnetism as to drive a sensitive person to drink or drugs to escape the mental and emotional pain he is experiencing.

There are many other forms of malpractice involving collective minds focusing their minds on one individual, and being entirely unconscious of its devastating effects. These few examples are given to help you discern such malpractice in your experience and that of others. It is important to be aware of this form of malpractice, for unless the victim understands that he is meeting collective malpractice, he may not be able to rise above its effects. It can cause him to become a failure, a drop-out from society, a runaway from home, to go on drugs, or even commit suicide.

Collective Malpractice from World Thought

Collective personal malpractice can take place on a very personal level, among family, friends, relatives. Each one's experience with it is unique. But there is another type of collective malpractice which is basically the same for all of humanity.

This is the collective malpractice which comes from world thought. The entire world believes in the reality of matter and evil. The mass belief in certain material laws, such as heredity, age, disease, death, is a form of mass hypnosis that becomes part of the mind of everyone.

Each person absorbs the culture in which he lives. Those mortal beliefs within consciousness seem necessary in order to relate to the culture around him, and he comes under the hypnotic suggestions present in it.

This collective thought in turn generates epidemics. Contagious illnesses, for example, are mental — a form of spreading hypnotic suggestions that flow from mind to mind to mind. The fear generated from seeing or hearing about the symptoms of flu, for example, will increase until we begin to manifest these symptoms and come down with flu. Economic depression is often mass hypnosis — the fear created by predictions of impending economic decline. The general world belief in age can cause us to decline into decrepitude.

This does not mean that the world is all one mass of destructive hypnotic influence. There is great good taking place in this age. This good is increasing daily as the Adam-dream continues to break up. But there is still present, and also growing, the collective mesmerism of the masses.

Until present times, universal hypnotic influence was not so aggressive. Today, animal magnetism is broadcast throughout the world in the unrelenting malpractice of the media. The limited spreading of mesmerism of the past, has become a flood of aggressive mental suggestion, amounting to mass hypnosis.

We voluntarily consent to this malpractice when we open our minds to the media, and absorb the news, fiction and real life drama of mortal mind. The media has a hypnotic effect on the public that is either ignorant, fraudulent or malicious. From advertising, to news, to drama, to advice and opinion, the media pours forth mental images that forcefully promotes the belief in the reality of evil and matter. Thus it negatively influences and forms the collective thought of the world we live in. In the ever-changing state of world consciousness, the media releases a constant miasma of false beliefs that mesmerizes the culture in which it is operating.

When we voluntarily accept its hypnotic appeal, we become victims of the mental pollution that contaminates the minds of millions. We should give serious consideration to the need to defend the mind from the mass hypnotism of the media.

Television, movies, radio, magazines, newspapers and books, implant vivid images of sickness and suffering in the undefended mind. Fiction and drama portray to the most minute detail violence

51

and sensualism. Non-fiction exploits shocking, graphic details of man's inhumanity to man. The medical profession and drug companies picture and describe sickness and disease, and promote the power of drugs to heal. The news emphasizes and exaggerates the most negative events taking place. Advertisements promote products and services that fall short of all that was claimed for them

The printed and spoken word of the media comes across as absolute fact. Dramas are enacted so convincingly that they appear to be true. Their message is presented with such conviction that it impresses upon us the seeming reality of mortal mind.

This flood of animal magnetism has a direct bearing on spiritual healing. When we absorb animal magnetism in such concentrated doses, it becomes increasingly real to us. It materializes and darkens the mind. If it enters consciousness on a regular basis and accumulates within, it hardens the inner self, for evil appears to be a power greater than God. The harmful effects of such negative 'realism' becomes a form of self-hypnosis, in which we build up in our own mind specific beliefs which we fear. These are then manifested outwardly in discord and disease. Such claims are hard to overcome because the mind is convinced they are real.

If we let evil influence us with such graphic images of sin and disease, these images remain with us for weeks, months, even years. As they accumulate, they put out our spirituality, and darken thought. This hardened mental state prevents the development of spiritual understanding upon which healing depends. A long build-up of dark, materialistic images shuts out the Christ-consciousness, and can retard, or totally obstruct, healing. Our emotional reactions to these images can even be the cause of sickness, disease and discord.

The human mind seems to have a certain fascination with evil. The media is magnetic. We are impressed and entertained by the audacity, violence, and seductiveness of animal magnetism. It is aggressive, sensual, shocking, clever, manipulative, and subtle, in trying to make us believe that it is real.

We cannot watch the godless propaganda of the media without reacting to it, analyzing it, fearing it, being disturbed by it, fretting and fuming over the irrational and violent acts of evil taking place. In so doing, we make a reality of evil, and become part of the mass hypnosis produced by the media. When we open our minds to this mental poison, we are on the same mental plane as the worldly-minded. We become mesmerized by animal magnetism, and when a claim arises, we have no reservoir of spirituality within to turn to.

If we are serious students of Christian Science, we must surely realize that we have a choice to make as to whether we are going to spiritualize consciousness, or be pulled into the mire of animal magnetism's mesmeric influence. Mrs. Eddy writes in *Miscellaneous Writings*, "Between the centripetal and centrifugal mental forces of material and spiritual gravitations, we go into or we go out of materialism and sin, and choose our course and its results. Which, then, shall be our choice,— the sinful, material, and perishable; or the spiritual, joy-giving, and eternal?" We cannot be moving in both directions at once. If we want to realize the healing and protection that is ours in Christian Science, we must separate ourselves from the material world as much as possible.

In analyzing personal and collective malpractice, it would appear that we are very much at the mercy of the minds of others. But we learn in Christian Science that all malpractice must become self-malpractice before it can affect us. If we think in the world's image of crime, dishonesty, war, bad weather, sickness, overweight, accidents, lack, lust, conflict and stress, if we accept the belief that evil and matter are real, then we malpractice on our own world, and image forth the mortal dream as our life.

In a society greatly shaped by the media, there is an unrelieved transference of hypnotic suggestion that goes from mind to mind to mind. When you listen to someone describe his or her illness, or gossip maliciously, or you see a commercial of a man taking cold, all the thoughts depicting each mental image have been transferred to your mind. They have malpracticed on your health, your life, your world.

Malpractice harms us only because we have consented to its influence. We usually do this unconsciously. An aggressive mental suggestion presents itself, and because of our belief in the reality of evil and matter, we accept it, react to it, and so make a reality of it. At some point the suggestion becomes a solid conviction. Even though the aggressive mental suggestion may have ceased talking to us, it has been converted into a form of self-malpractice which is planted in consciousness as a conviction that we continue to believe in.

To give several simple examples: A friend describes in every detail how his home was broken into and robbed, how shocked and devastated he was by this. His graphic description of the robbery, perhaps rehearsed several times, along with his emotional reactions, will initiate in us a fear and dread of being robbed — and this becomes a habit of self-malpractice. Even after we no longer hear about the friend's robbery, the fear and dread of it will haunt us. If we hold in consciousness such discordant experiences and fear that they could happen to us, then our fears may be imaged forth in the form of some kind of robbery.

Another example: We may see on TV a graphic description of back trouble — how it is caused, what goes wrong, even the suggestion that it is incurable, or could require an operation. We take in this ignorant, but malicious, malpractice, and become concerned that we may do something to hurt our back. Unless we handle the fear and free our consciousness of it, we could malpractice ourselves into this claim.

By such simple examples, we can see how the world is drowning in every kind of malpractice. For refuge from this onslaught of aggressive mental suggestion, we turn to Christian Science. When we do not know of Christian Science, the mortal material view is the only view. But as we study Christian Science, we also have a spiritual view, and so we have a choice, for we can make a distinct separation between good and evil, God and animal magnetism; we can determine if the thoughts we are entertaining express the Christ-consciousness or the antichrist. We can choose to have only the spiritual view. Our study of Christian Science gives us the insight to discern one from the other. Then we can control thought, claim our dominion over evil, and refuse to let it affect us. In so doing, we are protected from all forms of personal malpractice.

The Christ Consciousness — The Way Out

Lest we feel we can be helplessly victimized by the thoughts of others, I want to share here the scientific means through which we can prevent this. I quote here from Bicknell Young's paper titled "The Christ Consciousness." In it he writes of his first day in having Christian Science class instruction with Edward A. Kimball:

> When Mr. Kimball came on the platform the first day, at the time when I studied, he said something like this: "If I seem to manifest any physical discord, (and he seemed to) it is because many persons believe I am in error." He said that many persons had wanted to be in class and had not been permitted, and they believed him to be in great error.
>
> Would that mean that what those persons were believing had produced the physical discord? No — but it did seem that the belief entertained by a great many people seemingly was disturbing his thinking until his disturbed thinking about what they were thinking was objectified as physical discord . . .

What needed to be treated? Not simply that he was in error, but the claim that this belief, that he was in error, could disturb or harass him, or make him believe in what they were thinking, or fear what they were doing, or in any way hinder him or affect his thinking.

This was the claim — that what they were thinking could have some effect upon him, and thereby his own thinking be externalized as his physical body in some discordant phenomena. <u>The claim about what he thought about what they thought was the only claim to be healed. Now this is what we call malpractice.</u> The malpractice so-called could affect him only as his own thinking and in no other way.

Then what was he to do? His work was to maintain his own thinking, the Christ-consciousness, undisturbed and uninfluenced by the thoughts of others, by the thoughts that were arguing to him about what others were doing or thinking. (Science and Health 306:25) Paul said, "None of these things move me."

Even if the whole world believed him in error, this malpractice, these aggressive mental suggestions about him, could not make him think erroneously and so produce so-called physical ills and so make him seem to believe in error. These aggressive mental suggestions could not do a thing to his Christ-consciousness. Knowing this, the physical discords vanished quickly . . .

There is no other way under heaven whereby we can be saved except by the Christian Science method — by maintaining the Christ-consciousness that cannot be mesmerized by aggressive mental suggestions.

Chapter V

THE MALPRACTICE OF PROFESSIONAL HYPNOTISTS

Personal malpractice is part of our daily experience. Such events are not deliberate acts of hypnotism. Rather, they are ignorant and common forms of thought transference. As we progress in Christian Science, such malpractice becomes increasingly easy to detect and counteract.

Beyond these common forms of malpractice, is the malicious malpractice of those who deliberately practice hypnotism. The hypnotic work of a trained hypnotist is premeditated. It is the domination of one mortal will over another through highly developed mental powers. It is the essence of the antichrist, for it is capable of all evil.

After centuries of being shrouded in a mystic aura, the practice of hypnotism has become a specifically defined knowledge, freely available to everyone.

Until recent times, the average person going about his business, was not likely to be a target of secret hypnotic work; but today, the power of secret hypnosis, subliminal suggestion, and mental manipulation, has become so well known and so widely practiced, that it is a growing threat to individual freedom and self-government. In Christian Science, we can learn to recognize and handle the effects of secret hypnosis in order to be free of the mental control of the amoral mentality.

A trained hypnotist is the antitheses of a Christian Science practitioner. He can control and harm his victim as surely as a practitioner can heal and regenerate his patient. Although this destructive mental power is becoming more widely known and used, it is also being brought out into the open and exposed for the antichrist it is. Much has been written on how to hypnotize. There are also those who have written on the disastrous, even lethal, effects of hypnotism. And this brings us again to the urgency of establishing a means for protecting the mind from such mental powers.

A professional hypnotist can control the unsuspecting mind, as well as the mind that willingly submits to him. We will touch now on the various forms of malicious hypnotism, and list some of the symptoms or effects produced by secret hypnosis.

Reference:

> Animal magnetism, in its ascending steps of evil, entices its victim by unseen, silent arguments. Reversing the modes of good, in their silent allurements to health and holiness, it impels mortal mind into error of thought, and tempts into the committal of acts foreign to the natural inclinations. The victims lose their individuality, and lend themselves as willing tools to carry out the designs of their worst enemies, even those who would induce their self-destruction. Animal magnetism fosters suspicious distrust where honor is due, fear where courage should be strongest, reliance where there should be avoidance, a belief in safety where there is most danger; and these miserable lies, poured constantly into his mind, fret and confuse it, spoiling that individual's disposition, undermining his health, and sealing his doom, unless the cause of the mischief is found out and destroyed.
>
> Other minds are made dormant by it, and the victim is in a state of semi-individuality, with a mental haziness which admits of no intellectual culture or spiritual growth. The state induced by this secret evil influence is a species of intoxication, in which the victim is led to believe and do what he would never, otherwise, think or do voluntarily. (My 211)

The Occult

The earliest practice of hypnotism is found in the occult. The practice of occultism is not a special gift, but a form of knowledge that has been passed down through the ages.

The black arts are an exercise in evil. They are the work of moral idiocy, of a godless mind that can be unmerciful in the use of its mental powers. Voodoo, witchcraft, black magic, and Satanism are forms of intensified malicious hypnosis. Those who practice these forms of evil, intentionally project violent evil thoughts that cause a victim to suffer, be in pain or die. Those given to such vicious forms of hypnotism are motivated by the lowest elements of mortal emotions — depraved will-power, hate, revenge, a desire to control others and make them suffer, and satisfaction in doing so.

Over the centuries, the secrets of the occult were closely guarded, but today such hypnotic power is openly taught and practiced. Libraries and bookstores provide books on how to practice mind control and hypnotism. There are stores that specialize in voodoo and black magic; programs on television explore the practice of witchcraft, dramatize it, and present documentaries on it; classes are given in hypnotism. Learning hypnotism can easily lead to the practice of the black arts, if the mind tends in that direction.

For all that has been written on how to practice hypnotism, little has been given on how to detect and protect the mind from it. Most instructions on hypnotism warn of the lethal power in its misuse; but needless to say, this does not prevent it from being used for cruel and evil ends.

Included in the occult are astrology, numerology, palmistry, psychic powers, fortune-telling, etc. These ancient forms of mental influence play upon the belief in the mystic powers of the mind.

References:

Occultism cannot know to hinder the work of God, good. Occultism cannot embody itself mentally or physically. It cannot rob, steal, persecute, annoy, or destroy me or mine, for there is no occultism. (DC p 71)

The malicious mental argument and its action on the mind of the perpetrator, is fatal, morally and physically. From the effects of mental malpractice the subject scarcely awakes in time, and must suffer its full penalty after death. This sin against divine Science is canceled only through human agony: the measure it has meted must be remeasured to it.

The crimes committed under this new *regime* of mind-power, when brought to light, will make stout hearts quail. Its mystery protects it now, for it is not yet known. Error is more abstract than Truth. Even the healing Principle, whose power seems inexplicable, is not so obscure; for this is the power of God, and good should seem more natural than evil. (Mis 222)

A mental assassin's treatment of No, which is the thought of a person thinking No to every thought of you, results in a complete nullifying of what you are trying to do. The No treatment is a blanket and results in blankness and thoughtlessness.

Mrs. Eddy said, "The power of Mind fully understood is the ability to discern whether the thoughts you entertain are your own, or someone else's."

Hypnosis in the Name of Religion

While those using black magic and witchcraft make no pretense to having a moral or spiritual purpose to their work, other more subtle and sophisticated forms of hypnosis are found in Oriental metaphysics, Hinduism, theosophy, Roman Catholicism — especially Jesuitism. Here the work of trained hypnotists is often performed in the name of religion. Once again, the practice of hypnotic control is secretive, and takes on the aura of mysticism and the supernatural. When it is related to a religious organization, those who practice it may believe they are doing so as a spiritual calling. Thus, anathemas, curses, and many forms of malicious malpractice, are performed in the name of God, or a sacred cause.

Hypnosis, practiced on followers of a cult with its so-called spiritual leader, is done in the name of religion. The minds of the believers are easily hypnotized and controlled because of their faith in God, and willingness to obey a leader's mental influence. They offer no resistance to the hypnotism of a priest, or a guru. Their minds are totally undefended to the aggressive mental suggestions of the one in control. Such strong, unresisted malpractice can be as destructive as any practiced by the black arts, because the mal-practitioner believes he is leading his followers as a moral obliga-tion to God, and they obey for the same reason. The religious hypnotist will mesmerize his followers, and maintain a hold on them, through their fear or ignorance. At the same time, he may mali-ciously malpractice those he considers an enemy of his cult, or a threat to his control. Quite often it is hypnotism that holds a cult together.

We need to be aware that such hypnotism is being prac-ticed, because it is done so silently and secretly. Whether occult or religious in nature, the hypnotist does his work with no warning to the victim that it is taking place.

Most deceiving is the malpractitioner who goes to great lengths to become a close and trusted friend of a Christian Scien-tist. Such a malpractitioner hides himself behind a mask of inno-cence, friendship, and even a spiritual kinship. This duplicity is carefully cultivated to keep the subject off guard, trusting, and open to aggressive mental suggestions from him. If we have a problem that does not heal, we should consider the background of those close to us, and quietly handle malpractice from anyone suspected of being capable of it. If there is a change in the claim, we have usually identified the source.

We should not assume, because a metaphysical or religious system claims to practice Christianity, that it is beyond the use of malicious hypnosis to achieve its ends, control its believers, or destroy its enemies.

Religious organizations and secret societies that have practiced hypnotism in the past, are just as active in doing so today. We cannot be too careful in avoiding involvement with them, for those in control of such organizations and societies recognize the power of Christian Science to annul their hypnotic work, and protect the mind from their control; they feel this threat as keenly today as they did in Mrs. Eddy's time. In fact, their secret, mental malpractice against Christian Scientists undoubtedly has contributed more to the decline of the movement than any other factor. It is possible that the sudden demise of a dedicated worker in the Christian Science movement is the result of the secret hypnotic work of those who want to see Christian Science forever buried and forgotten.

One must even be aware of the malpractice in the Christian Science organization. When the position or reputation of a so-called Christian Scientist is threatened by another in the Church, he may resort to malpractice — perhaps assuming that he is properly treating and protecting himself from an attack by animal magnetism. The perversion of mental work by some who call themselves Christian Scientists, is not a thing of the past. There are times when a stubborn claim has been met by handling the malpractice of a misguided Christian Scientist who has been disobeyed or defied by a another, or whose ambitions have been threatened or thwarted by another in the organization. It seems essential that this abuse of mental power by Christian Scientists should be brought to light. There are times when one's suffering and pain comes from those in his own household.

References:

From ordinary mental practice to Christian Science is a long ascent, but to go from the use of inanimate drugs to any susceptible misuse of the human mind, such as mesmerism, hypnotism, and the like, is to subject mankind unwarned and undefended to the unbridled individual human will. The currents of God flow through no such channels.

The whole world needs to know that the milder forms of animal magnetism are yielding to its more aggressive features. We have no moral right and no authority in Christian Science for influencing the thoughts of others, except it be to serve God and benefit mankind. Man is properly self-governed, and he should be guided by no other mind than Truth, the divine Mind. Christian Science gives neither moral right nor might to harm either man or beast. The Christian Scientist is alone with his own being and with the reality of things. The mental malpractitioner is not, cannot be, a Christian Scientist; he is disloyal to God and man; he has every opportunity to mislead the human mind, and he uses it. People may listen complacently to the suggestion of the inaudible falsehood, not knowing what is hurting them or that they are hurt. This mental bane could not bewilder, darken, or misguide consciousness, physically, morally, or spiritually, if the individual knew what was at work and his power over it.

This unseen evil is the sin of sins; it is never forgiven. Even the agony and death that it must sooner or later cause the perpetrator, cannot blot out its effects on himself till he suffers up to its extinction and stops practising it. The crimes committed under this new-old regime of necromancy or diabolism are not easily reckoned. At present its mystery protects it, but its hidden modus and flagrancy will finally be known, and the laws of our land will handle its thefts, adulteries, and murders, and will pass sentence on the darkest and deepest of human crimes.

Christian Scientists are not hypnotists, they are not mortal mind-curists, nor faith-curists; they have faith, but they have

Science, understanding, and works as well. They are not the *addenda*, the *etceteras*, or new editions of old errors; but they are what they are, namely, students of a demonstrable Science leading the ages. (Message for 1901 p 19)

Catholicism is brotherly love, while Roman Catholicism is the Pope's intention. Roman Catholicism is a false conception of true theology. No cloister, circles, Jesuitism, priesthood, Papal power or school of cardinals or bishops can be a channel through which mortal mind can work or rule my consciousness or the consciousness of any individual to bind or hold you, or him, through ignorance, fear, or superstition.

No Roman Catholic prayer or prophecy or anathema nor curse can dim, deaden, darken, or confuse your consciousness, nor blur the Christ image in your thought. There is no God in any prayer of condemnation — no Christ in it — no Truth in it, and therefore there is no *power* in it and *you cannot fear it.* There is no power or rule or government or control apart from God. There is no power or belief of power that can hinder you from any right achievement. Remember your efficiency and capacity are unlimited, and no effort of evil to reverse the words and works of Christian Science can hinder your success. All ability, all achievement, all accomplishment are possible to men because they are man's. It is the law of man's being from which he cannot escape even if he would, to know all that God, Mind, includes and is. (DC p 75)

Hypnosis as an Alternative Healing Method

Hypnosis is included among alternative healing methods presently gaining recognition. However, it is generally acknowledged that hypnosis does not really heal. The use of hypnosis for healing has proven no more effective today than in times past, for it does not remove the mental cause of a problem. It may draw from the subconscious some clue as to what needs to be treated, but it has no power to actually free the mind of the mental disturbance. Actually, hypnotism is the exercise of will-power in which the stronger mentality hypnotizes the patient into a temporary change of mind. The hypnotist's suggestions override the victim's own thoughts and feelings, but they never reach or heal the real cause of the problem. At best, hypnosis offers a temporary relief. As the hypnotic trance wears off, the problem reasserts itself, sometimes having grown worse during the hypnotic period.

Moreover, while in a trance, one does not know what the hypnotist will suggest to him. He assumes it will be only good, positive, beneficial thoughts, but the transference — even unconsciously — of the hypnotist's negative or harmful thoughts is not only possible, but most likely. Thus it is dangerous to surrender the control of one's mind to another, for he cannot always know what thoughts the hypnotist will implant in his mind.

The purpose of Mesmer's work and that of other early hypnotists, was to relieve suffering. In the alternative healing of today, there can be no doubt that many who practice hypnotism have the same humanitarian purpose in mind. Their intent is benign; but even thorough investigation of it in recent years, has not given to hypnotism any lasting healing power.

References:

Mesmerism will smile and be pleasant and all the while doing some mischief. Good is All. Evil is not mind, has no intelligence, is powerless and falls by its own weight. (DC p 10)

The mental stages of crimes, which seem to belong to the latter days, are strictly classified in metaphysics as some of the many features and forms of what is properly denominated, in extreme cases, moral idiocy. . .

This mental disease at first shows itself in extreme sensitiveness; then, in a loss of self-knowledge and of self-condemnation, — a shocking inability to see one's own faults, but an exaggerating sense of other people's. Unless this mental condition be overcome, it ends in a total loss of moral, intellectual, and spiritual discernment, and is characterized in this Scripture: "The fool hath said in his heart, There is no God." This state of mind is the exemplification of total depravity, and the result of sensuous mind in matter. Mind that is God is not in matter; and God's presence gives spiritual light, wherein is no darkness. . . .

Whoever is mentally manipulating human mind, and is not gaining a higher sense of Truth by it, is losing in the scale of moral and spiritual being, and may be carried to the depths of perdition by his own consent. He who refuses to be influenced by any but the divine Mind, commits his way to God, and rises superior to suggestions from an evil source. Christian Science shows that there is a way to escape from the latter-day ultimatum of evil, through scientific truth; and so all are without excuse. (Mis p 113)

Use of Hypnosis by Governments

Most people will never come in contact with the most sophisticated and aggressive forms of secret hypnosis now practiced — that used by the power struggle among nations. But enough has been written about it as first hand experience to show that hypnosis is used without any moral restraint among governments in order to assure their hold on power, to guard their nation's security, and to spy on other nations.

The study and use of hypnosis by the government is malicious, and even lethal. While the government's use of hypnosis has been documented to some extent, it is likely that no one will ever know exactly how it has been used to shape events, and control officials at all levels of government. The power of secret hypnosis can wrongly influence the decisions of government officials including Supreme Court justices, senators, congressmen, the President and his Cabinet. It is possible that hypnotic control could account for the confusion, indecision, and lack of leadership that comes about after an official takes office. A trained hypnotist can silently transmit suggestions to his or her mind, and unless the subject is aware that this mental transference is taking place, he will believe the thoughts and decisions and actions are his own.

Such aggressive mental suggestion is a mental power exercised by those trained in hypnosis. It is within reason to assume that they can project a decision, or plan, or idea they want a victim to act on, and suddenly he will find himself saying or doing something he had no intention of saying or doing, and it will seem to be his own decision even to himself, unless he reflects on what has happened, and detects that he is being mentally manipulated.

Those who work in high level security and decision making positions, are faced with the threat of such mental manipulation daily. Unless they are Christian Scientists, they have no sure way of defending their minds from the collective malpractice of those who want to influence them erroneously.

Even more disturbing, is the use of hypnosis by government agencies who can, through brainwashing, program a subject to kill on command through the use of post-hypnotic suggestion. A subject can be programmed to receive a secret command, revert to a second personality, and in this robot-like state, carry out a criminal act, even assassination, and then turn that violence upon himself and commit suicide. Professional hypnotists can also block out memories, and implant false memories in their place. They can change or alter the mind, behavior, and memory of the victim at subconscious or unconscious levels.

There are instances when important government officials and military commanders have either died suddenly or committed suicide, for no apparent reason. Such deaths seem mysterious to those unaware of the lethal powers of hypnotism. It is possible that those who have been taken out by hypnotic attack, were meeting the collective malicious malpractice of professional hypnotists. When one is suddenly aggressively mentally attacked by two or more malicious hypnotists at once, the victim has little hope of escaping the fatal effects of such concentrated malice — outside of Christian Science.

I touch on professional hypnotism to show how its use is now at all levels of the Western world.

I have not explored at great length the many forms of professional hypnotism practiced today. There is much information available on it through book stores and libraries. We do need to be aware that mind control is being widely practiced. But I have found that an in-depth knowledge of any use of hypnotism is extremely detrimental to spiritual healing.

During the years in which I was a Christian Science practitioner, I had some patients ask for help for serious physical problems. I could not seem to reach them. I then learned that they had studied, or were studying, Far Eastern religions and other mystical metaphysics. Consciously or subconsciously they were always trying to mix Christian Science with these other studies. More than once they insisted that there was no basic difference between Far Eastern mysticism and Christian Science. Because their mind had been so darkened by their study of Oriental mysticism, I could not reach them and heal them. Other practitioners have had the same experience with patients who have studied Far Eastern religions.

This illustrates the extremely serious threat to the demonstration of Christian Science found in a study of the teachings and methods of any form of occultism, hypnotism, mysticism, Hinduism, or Orientalism. The study of Christian Science will equip the student to detect and protect his mind from all foreign influence, including malicious malpractice and the Far Eastern religions. This protection is best when we have no knowledge of what they teach.

As complex as the knowledge about hypnotism has become, the effects of malicious malpractice are basically the same, whatever the source. Its purpose — to control the mind — makes it sinister in motive. It is nothing less than the work of moral idiocy. When used as a healing agent, it may have a benign motive, but the results have not proven to be good. Deliberate or premeditated malpractice can mentally cripple, or even kill, the innocent person.

While we do not study hypnosis or practice it, we should be aware of the effects it has on the inner self. For then, should we come under mental attack, we can recognize what's handling us, and keep it from doing so.

At one time it was too frightening to explore these facts about hypnosis with Christian Scientists. A century ago, Scientists were living in a world innocent of the far-reaching power of hypnotism. But the time has come when we can and must be educated in the effects of malicious hypnosis in order to handle it for ourselves and the world. As we do, we will prevent the "Reign of Terror" foreseen by Mrs. Eddy.

References:

No mortal thought put in action by any mesmerist, or combined force of mesmerists, or anyone whom they should employ, has any power to affect.

There is no M.A.M. "The Lord He is God and there is none beside Him." Prov. 16: 7. (DC p 186)

Never fear the mental malpractitioner, the mental assassin, who, in attempting to rule mankind, tramples upon the divine Principle of metaphysics, for God is the only power. (S&H p 419)

Also the teacher must thoroughly fit his students to defend themselves against sin, and to guard against the attacks of the would-be *mental assassin*, who attempts to kill morally and physically. No hypothesis as to the existence of another power should interpose a doubt or fear to hinder the demonstration of Christian Science. (S&H p 445)

There is no educated mortal mind through hatred of the Truth, or through jealousy, that can hypnotize me into believing that there is any reality outside of God, Love. (DC p 81)

It is always right to obey the scripture and when converted to strengthen the brethren. But there is great wisdom to be used in knowing just how much to say, and when to say it. I recommend that the C. S. Jour. preserve a wise reticence on this subject until the world is more enlightened on the awful error of mental malpractice, or Malicious An. Mag. There will be a time when it can be, must be, met and laid bare before the people. But my dear Students show themselves not quite equal yet to meeting this question silently or audibly just as it can be met and thus destroyed to each one's own consciousness. This is done not by a sense that there is no such evil in claim, but only that there is no such evil in reality; just as sin or sickness is to be considered. Love is the victor over all. (DC p 120)

Symptoms and Effects of Hypnotic Influence

The malpractice of professional hypnotists can create many different effects. All of the symptoms or effects attributed to malpractice listed in the previous chapter also apply to malicious malpractice. But the hypnotic work of trained hypnotists can prove to be much more challenging and difficult to counteract.

The victim can be made to believe he has a malignant condition such as leukemia, a tumor on the brain or elsewhere in the body. If hypnotists silently suggest to him, day and night, a cancerous belief, he will begin to believe it, fear it, imagine he has the disease, and then produce it on his own body. During such hypnotic attacks, his head may be in great pain and his mind confused.

This attack can be met by carefully determining that the claim is not originating in one's own mind, but is being suggested to him from outside sources. Establishing this fact, he can then decide that it is not *his* thought, and so he can ignore and reject the suggestion until it ceases 'speaking' to him. He should also read works on Christian Science and "pray without ceasing," until he no longer hears the suggestion.

Colds and flu may be caused by malicious malpractice. When one manifests the symptoms of either, he should handle malpractice vigorously. Often these claims can be met quickly by recognizing that they are not the effect of physical causes, but of malpractice.

Malpractice can create deep depression, even manic depression. Such depression can cause the victim to commit suicide, or pass on, for no apparent reason. Deep depression alone is enough to render one incapable of thinking clearly. When one is overcome with depression and excruciating headaches, this could be due to malicious malpractice.

Extreme sexual desire can be caused by malpractice. An unrelieved obsession with sex is abnormal and can be the result of the hypnotic work of enemies using one's sexual desires as an avenue through which to handle him.

Trained hypnotists can cause a painful foot condition known as foot podding, so that walking is very difficult.

If the hypnotist knows his victim has a physical claim, he will work to intensify the claim, and make it appear incurable. He will argue that Christian Science does not heal, and he will reverse healings that have taken place, causing the claim to return. When a healing is recent, it can be more easily reversed. Thus the need to protect a healing until enough time has passed for it to be firmly established.

Hypnotists often attack at night when the victim is asleep. The mind is easier to reach when it is unconscious and undefended. If the attack is especially vicious, the victim can have terrifying nightmares. If it is unusual to have nightmares, they can certainly be due the result of hypnotic attack. One may awake in the middle of the night overwhelmed with the sense of guilt, self-condemnation, and self-incrimination, or of terror, or of depression and futility, for no apparent reason. If such emotions are not present during the day, but are extremely aggressive at night, this would indicate malpractice.

One may awaken in the night aware that some hypnotic suggestion of an incurable disease is being implanted in consciousness. If one awakens with the distinct impression that his mind is being attacked, he should get up and do good prayerful work to clear his mind before going to sleep again. If one senses that there are hypnotic attacks often taking place during the night, he should not go to bed, but stay up and do prayerful work for himself before retiring. Several nights of diligent metaphysical work should stop the hypnotic attack.

An extremely vicious attack, during the day as well as the night, can cause the victim to experience waves of terror, or have a dreadful premonition that something terrible is going to happen to him. He may feel overwhelmed with waves of terror for no reason. He may also feel very dark and void of spiritual inspiration, as though separated from God. During these attacks he should do as little human activity as possible, stay quiet, and do much prayerful work for himself.

There is no way to describe the mental pain and agony that such hypnotic attacks can cause, and the dreadful effects they have for some time after the attack is over. The effects of such attacks do not fade out immediately once they cease, but may require time to wear off.

Mrs. Eddy was greatly concerned over the threat of mentally administered poison, and she urged her students to handle mental and electrical poison. Such poisons should still be handled. Electrical poison is the transference to a victim of negative energy driven by malice, hate, envy and jealousy. At such times, the victim seems to have little control over his own thoughts. Electrical poison can produce an attack of nerves, and the victim cannot remain quiet and think clearly.

Mental poison can be the cause of death, if the poison administered mentally is not handled in Christian Science. Mental poison can also cause physical claims such as poor eyesight, painful condition in teeth and gums, heart attack, and extreme fatigue.

One form of malpractice seems to attack at night. It is a violent suggestion that there is no God, that God does not exist, that He has never existed. This malicious malpractice can be so intensely aggressive as to make one doubt the existence of God.

It is possible that malicious malpractice can cause a person to lose control of his mind and appear to be insane or commit suicide.

Malpractice can also cause adverse conditions and discordant relationships that make one's life extremely difficult. It can destroy his home and marriage, turn friends and neighbors against him, or cause him to lose his source of income. Such mental attacks can claim to destroy his health, home and property with no indication as to the real cause of such adversity. The world attributes it to fate, or chance, or circumstances, but the work of malicious malpractice should be thoroughly handled if such events begin to take place.

There are undoubtedly many other effects brought about by trained hypnotists. Those listed here are intended to give some clue as to the most difficult challenges one meets from their malicious work.

All of these forms of malpractice may be frightening to consider — unless one knows that they are malpractice. Knowing this, he knows they are not his own thoughts, but hypnotic suggestions that can be overcome in Christian Science.

It is wise, if possible, to avoid personal contact with anyone who is suspected of practicing hypnotism — especially if the person knows one is a Christian Scientist. From Mrs. Eddy's time to the present, most cult leaders, Far Eastern religionists, Theosophists, the clergy of the Roman Catholic Church, and others who practice mind control, recognize that Christian Science is the one power that can protect the mind from hypnotic control. The secretive nature of their hypnotic work makes it inadvisable to offer them the opportunity to contact our mind directly — especially when their knowledge of secret hypnotism and post hypnotic suggestion, is something we are not experienced in handling.

I strongly advise the experienced Scientist who is meeting malpractice, never to let anyone else know about it — especially the one suspected of being the source of it. The Scientist should appear to be totally unaffected by the hypnotist's work. If a hypnotist knows his work is being effective, he will work with more determination to achieve his ends. But if he thinks his work is having no effect, he will finally stop. A hypnotist works secretly, never showing his true colors, and so the victim should also work secretly in defending himself.

Many strange experiences of those who have visited the Far East and come under the spell of a trained Eastern hypnotist, are enough to warn the Scientist to beware of an encounter with these mentalities. I have noticed that Scientists who travel to the Far East and become submerged in the mesmeric atmosphere of millions of minds believing in the Far Eastern religions, often find their spiritual light dimmed or temporarily lost because of the overwhelming darkness of the Oriental mind.

Because of the growing use of hypnotism, I must make the following statement. It is one that Scientists often find shocking and incredible, but it is true: There are forms of malicious malpractice so strong and aggressive that even an experienced Christian Scientist cannot counteract and overcome them. This is due to the power of the malicious work of the hypnotist, which is taking place in a world consciousness so mortal and materialistic that it reinforces his negative mental work, while the Scientist lacks the spiritual development that equips him to counteract and nullify such malicious malpractice.

Our best protection from such malpractice comes from the spiritual intuitions that tell us not to make contact with certain mentalities in the first place. We learn to stay away from those whom we suspect of being into hypnosis in any form. If we are not able to overcome the malpractice directed towards us, the answer is to cut off all connections with him and put enough time and distance between ourselves and the malpractitioner that his hypnotic influence is not able to reach us.

It is not likely that a dedicated Christian Scientist and a malicious hypnotic mentality, should be forced into a permanent relationship. If we are working correctly in Science, God will deliver us from such malicious mental work by showing us the way to leave behind such relationships, or circumstances.

In the past, the majority of people never encountered such extreme malpractice as that of today's professional hypnotist. But now hypnotism is so widely known and practiced, that one can only be assured of protection from it if he can recognize its influence on him, and meet it with prayerful work in Christian Science.

The deeper we go into Christian Science, the more sensitive we are to the inner voice — the spiritual intuitions and divine ideas that signify the presence of God within. This sensitivity also applies to the thoughts of others. We can become extremely sensitive to the malice, anger, or hatred, coming from another, and the silent mental arguments and thought discussions another may be having with us. We can detect the presence of malicious malpractice, for the mind seems to be invaded by thoughts and feelings totally alien to our normal state of mind. Experience will enable you to know whether the thoughts you are entertaining are your own, or those coming from mortal mind, or those unfolding from the divine Mind.

The development of such sensitivity requires three things — an acknowledgment that malpractice takes place, a recognition of its symptoms, and an understanding of Christian Science that counteracts its influence, and prevents it from entering consciousness.

References:

Hypnotism cannot nauseate, irritate, cannot keep up nervous symptoms; cannot control organs or functions of the body. Deny claim of old age.

No sexual poison, no sexual disease to cause arsenical poison to act on the stomach, joints, muscles and nerve centers, as a specific curse. No curse able to cause diseased bones or disintegration of tissues. There are no electro-magnetic currents to convey poison to nerve centers or to send dispatches over the body physical or mental. (DC p 79)

Even a blind faith removes bodily ailments for a season, but hypnotism changes such ills into new and more difficult forms of disease. (S&H 375)

You, false claim of malicious mind, whatever or wherever you are, you cannot mesmerize me, or hypnotize me to think I haven't understanding to meet any claim that comes to me. (DC p 81)

The law of divine Life, Truth and Love is a law of instant and complete expulsion and elimination of all poisons and impurities from the system. Why? Because the floodtides of divine Life, Truth and Love are pouring and surging through consciousness, uplifting, purifying, nourishing, healing, elevating, sustaining and energizing mankind. (DC p 73)

Neither mesmerism, hypnotism, theosophy, esoteric magic nor wicked mental or audible arguments can affect me. God governs me. Justice, Truth, Love, govern us, and nothing else can or does affect us in the least. (DC p 74)

Mental malpractice and malicious animal magnetism are utterly without power, and cannot voice error to me in the nature of arsenical, mercurial, electric, opium or any other poison or over-whelming soporific influence, mentally, physically, morally, or in any other way, for I am panoplied in divine Love where human hatred cannot reach me. Love, not hate; Truth, not error, govern man. (DC p 72)

WATCH - The claim of hypnotism, mesmerism, electro-magnet-ism, and animal magnetism, is that they work through nerves. Now let us cut their wires and know that there are no nerves. Mind does the talking and Mind is God. (DC p 38)

Malicious hypnotism cannot operate in my thought when I am asleep and manifest itself the next day as sin, disease and death. (DC p 82)

I rise in the strength of Spirit to resist all that is unlike God. I am spiritual; I feel, I know that I am one with Christ in God who hath all dominion.

There is no sin or error, to mesmerize me into seeing or feel-ing a body.

There is no malignant animal magnetism to prevent me from reflecting light.

There is no self-mesmerism to hide me from Truth, or Truth from me.

There is no hypnotism or mental malpractice to harm me, to affright me, touch me, for divine Love surrounds me. Intelligence, power, substance are the source of my being. Life enfolds me.

There is no motive power but God, no universe but Life, Truth and Love. There is no channel, nor channels, personal or impersonal, through or by which animal magnetism, either mali-cious, wilful, or ignorant, or sympathetic, conscious or uncon-scious, can approach Christian Science, its Discoverer, its adher-ents, or their patients. (DC p 69)

WATCH - Know that M.A.M. has no intelligence to make a law that mercurial or arsenical poison can be mentally administered to produce catarrhal condition of the body. God is the only lawmaker. There is no belief in a mentality through which poison can be hypnotically administered. (DC p 38)

WATCH - There is no fear and no thoughts of poison can come. There are no such thoughts.

There is no arsenic and no opiates producing any effect on anyone in this house and no one can be made to believe there is. Love reigns here.

Truth and Life eternal reign here and nothing else can come here.

There are no evil suggestions, no hypnotism, theosophy, no electro-magnetism. *God is All, etc.* (DC p 46)

Animal magnetism, hypnotism, spiritualism, theosophy, agnosticism, pantheism, and infidelity are antagonistic to true being and fatal to its demonstration; and so are some other systems. (S&H 129)

One more candid hint I will throw out on things less sacred, but very requisite. Give the mesmerists no points to your disadvantage. The wicked horde of this class in Boston exceed any other place. Never name (and caution your family also) any belief of sickness in the past or present; no private experiences of any sort unless they are good and true. (DC p 107)

Christian Scientists, be a law to yourselves that mental malpractice cannot harm you either when asleep or when awake. (S&H 442)

For further information on the handling of Roman Catholicism, see the Bookmark Collection entitled *Christian Science vs Roman Catholicism.*

Chapter VI

CHRISTIAN SCIENCE
THE ONE TRUE DEFENSE
AGAINST MALPRACTICE

The protection from malpractice found in Christian Science is not a simple formula, a quick and easy prayer that automatically shuts out all aggressive mental suggestion. Because the challenge is so complex and difficult, the answer is also demanding.

We find in Christian Science an escape and refuge from all evil, because this Science offers a *transcending view* of man and the universe. This view provides an alternative view to the present material one. As we develop the spiritual view, we also acquire the ability to handle malpractice.

To understand the significance of the spiritual view, we first need to analyze the present mortal, material view and its susceptibility to malpractice.

The Material View

With few exceptions, the collective thought we now live in has basically one concept of the universe and man — the mortal, material view. This view is based on the absolute conviction that evil and matter are real. Today we have a very material view of the universe and man — an image of a mortal man adrift in a godless universe, a helpless speck of life in a great black void of mindless space. We are told that chance and probability alone have somehow created the stars and the planets, man and all living things.

Each person believes without a doubt that evil is real, that matter is the medium in which he lives, and that his very being is at the mercy of material laws and unforeseen circumstances. The material view claims that *there is no absolute truth — everything is relative.* The latest theory now assumes that the entire basis of creation is one of total chaos. The mortal view is not only godless, but dark and hopeless — if one believes it to be true.

The material view, void of any spiritual light, is now producing a chaotic state in world consciousness, which is going through a period of extreme chemicalization. It is in this framework of false assumptions that malpractice operates. The mind, mesmerized by this false view, has no other view. Thus when malpractice — ignorant or malicious — causes sickness, disease, discord, or lack, the person blames his problems on virus, germs, age, chance or circumstances, the weather, the economy, etc. Because of this, he fails to heal such problems permanently, for he attributes them to material or evil causes over which he seems to have no control. So long as he blames his problems on such causes, he will not arrive at the true cause of his problems — his own conviction in evil as a power opposed to God.

The average mind, with a mixture of good and evil, is on the same plane as others like it, and so it cannot differentiate between its own thoughts and those coming from another. All thoughts are basically the same. This mind has no difficulty in relating to the mortal thoughts and emotions of similar minds. So long as the mind is darkened by the mortal view, so long as it believes in sin, disease and death, it is one with the hypnotic influence coming from the minds around it.

The world treats hypnotic power as a reality — a strong, aggressive thought force that competes with the forces of good, and overcomes the weak or undefended mind. Because the human mind, unenlightened by Christian Science, believes in the power of evil, and has no absolute right or wrong standard, it relates easily to hypnotic suggestion. It believes in sickness, disease, adversity, and so consents to the suggestion of them, and reacts emotionally to them. In fact, the human mind relates so totally to aggressive mental suggestion, that it cannot tell the difference between its own thoughts and those that are the malpractice of another.

The human mind can analyze animal magnetism, but it cannot overcome it. Even the prayer of faith and supplication has no lasting effect on it. Therefore, we must conclude that the human mind has little or no defense against the hypnotic influences of animal magnetism.

Unless we know about Christian Science, we are on the same mental level where transference of mortal thought goes on daily. We emit, as well as receive, various forms of malpractice. Hypnotic influence, entering consciousness, will often harden into conviction. A constant intake of aggressive mental suggestion, acts like an obstruction or wall between the inner self and God. While we seem innocent victims of malpractice, the fact is, we suffer from it because we govern our own thoughts and unconsciously consent to accepting false suggestions.

In the material view, malpractice becomes a real and powerful force, wherein we have the humanly good person fighting against the forces of evil. This suggests an unending battle, with no victory, no final peace, no real freedom for the person resisting evil through human goodness and will-power. At the heart of this struggle is the fact that, outside of Christian Science, there has not been established an absolute truth to use in resisting and defeating the lies of animal magnetism.

We have then a purely material view of creation resting on the conviction that matter and evil are real, claiming that there is no absolute truth, that all is relative, that ultimately the universe comes from a basis of chaotic energy. A mind fixed in this view is at one with the mortal beliefs in it, and has no certain means of defending itself from malpractice.

The Missing Cause

There is one great flaw in the structure of the material view — *the assumption that there is a final material or mindless cause to the universe and man.* The presence of this cause is assumed, for no material cause has ever been found. The origin of creation vanishes into a non-material dimension, which remains a mystery to the darkened mind.

This missing cause provides the opening we need to establish an entirely new view of creation and man — one based on Spirit, instead of matter. The human mind, reasoning from a material basis, sees in this realm only chaos, or utter darkness, from which chance and probability have created the universe and man. But Christian Science gives us a complete and accurate description of the structure and contents of this hidden dimension, and so provides an entirely different view of the universe and man — a transcending view. It brings to light a new knowledge, or advanced intelligence, about this hidden dimension, so that Christian Science becomes a bedrock of Truth to man. With this absolute Truth, we can distinguish between the real and the unreal, Spirit and matter, the hypnotic suggestions of animal magnetism and the spiritual ideas unfolding from the divine Mind filling the unseen realm. This absolute Truth, at the heart of consciousness, is our protection from the influence of animal magnetism.

This final Truth is not determined by the human mind; it is of God. It is first found in the Scriptures, the Ten Commandments, and the Sermon on the Mount. It has come in modern times as Christian Science — a scientific discovery that accurately defines the non-material realm beyond the five physical senses. This Science presents the correct view of God and man, revealing that they are not material, but spiritual.

Christian Science explains that life and the universe did not originate in chaos and chance, but came to light through the mani-

82

festation of divine intelligence, for all cause and effect belong to the one Mind; and so we have an intelligent cause to creation. This Science reveals the laws, elements, and qualities of the hidden realm. It is an education in spiritual realities that transforms our view of God and man. It is an absolute, never-changing foundation of Truth against which to measure all thoughts and feelings.

With Christian Science then, we have a choice of views. We can sink into the sands of mortal belief, or build on the rock of eternal Truth. Christian Science is an absolute Science that enables us to know the difference between good and evil, Truth and error, the spiritual ideas of divine Mind and the hypnotic suggestions of animal magnetism. It enables us to put out the material view by gradually purifying consciousness of all error, and establishing it in the Truth.

When we study Christian Science, we begin to develop an advanced intelligence that enables us to handle malpractice with authority. From the time we begin our study, we are learning to demesmerize consciousness, and protect it from hypnotic suggestion. Our mind shifts from the ever-changing illusions of animal magnetism to the spiritual rock of Truth and Love. We think differently from mesmeric world belief. Our protection from malpractice is in direct proportion to the spiritualization of thought.

Through study and prayer, we learn to detect and destroy the mortal state of mind. We see how world beliefs constantly malpractice on the Christ-consciousness within; and if we are wise, we take care as to what we accept into consciousness, and how much we allow the pictures of adversity, discord, and disease to impress us.

The Spiritual View

Christian Science is the opposite of the material viewpoint. It begins with the fact that God, good, is All-in-all, and evil and matter are powerless and unreal — illusions mesmerizing the human mind. In view of the aggressiveness of evil, the declaration that evil is unreal may seem an incredible statement; but if one tests it out in Christian Science, he finds it can be proven.

This revolutionary discovery that God is All, and evil and matter are unreal, is the basis for demonstrating Christian Science. It is the transcending view that eventually delivers us from the hypnotic influence of evil. Our defense against malpractice is based on the complete separation between God and animal magnetism. God alone is real, the only cause and creator, the origin of the universe and man. Christian Science declares that evil is neither person, place, nor thing. It does not exist as a reality. The human mind sees malicious animal magnetism as a reality, an evil intelligence and force that often appears more powerful than God. But as we develop the spiritual view, we gain the power to destroy evil. When we declare that God is All and evil is nothing, and understand the statements we are making, we not only establish a scientific fact, but we have all the power of God enforcing our prayerful work in proving it. We then see healing results, for evil and discord diminish and disappear. Each time we handle malpractice and overcome it, we increase our conviction that evil is indeed unreal and powerless.

Outside of Christian Science, we appear to be easily influenced by aggressive suggestions, but our belief in matter and evil, and the negative disposition this produces, is not our true being. We seem limited and finite because of the illusion that evil and matter are real. This belief seems to separate us from God.

In Christian Science, we learn that man in God's image cannot be influenced by animal magnetism, for he is one with God. God is cause, and man is effect. This oneness is a divine reality, and no mortal belief can destroy it. It is established and maintained by God. In *Science and Health*, Mrs. Eddy refers to "a divine influence ever present in the human consciousness." Through this indestructible oneness with God, we learn that we are not a helpless pawn in an immense mindless universe. We are the object of God's warm and tender care. We are not adrift in a sea of chance, fate and circumstances, but embraced in the Father's plan for us. This is not religious theory, but scientific fact. In Christian Science, we sense God's closeness, and realize that we are not alone, struggling against the forces of evil. Rather, God is working with us to lead us into a refuge and haven from the godless influence of animal magnetism.

Reference:

> When you argue on all subjects that should end well, be a law to your own consciousness that what you say cannot be reversed and inverted, and made to produce the very opposite of what you argue for. This is a late phase of theosophy and M.A.M. that needs to be met. (DC p 49)

Malpractice seems very real, threatening, and powerful to the material mind, and this fear alone gives it power over the mind that believes in it. But as God's presence and power become real to the mind in rapport with Him, this mind becomes fearless, knowing that it is protected from suggestions coming from animal magnetism. We need this feeling of God's nearness as we work out of the Adam-dream. Without Christian Science, we seem very much alone in the effort to overcome evil; but with Christian Science, we find the courage and strength to challenge animal magnetism and overcome it.

In this Science, the element of suggestibility used by animal magnetism to influence us, becomes the element of receptivity used by God to enlighten us. While hypnotic influence darkens the mind, the unfoldment of God's thoughts inspires and transforms it. As God's thoughts unfold within, they spiritualize consciousness. The more we spiritualize consciousness, the more astute we become in detecting and rejecting malpractice.

Christian Science is so vast and profound a discovery that we can only touch here on its fundamental teachings. The important thing is to make the spiritual view practical, to become so educated in its concepts that we can actually use it to deliver us from all evil. But to achieve this requires a long-term commitment to study and prayer.

Study and Prayer

Because malpractice is subjective, dominion over it is also subjective. It is a battle between truth and error within one's own mind. Dominion over evil involves far more than a faith-filled prayer to God for protection. We come now to the very heart of this discussion: The one thing that protects us from malpractice is *the consecrated study of Christian Science combined with the unique prayer of affirmation and denial, known as the Christian Science treatment.*

How does this work protect the mind? Evil influences the mind because of the mind's susceptibility to suggestion. Yet we cannot become insensitive to incoming thoughts, for this sensitivity is also the means through which God's thoughts reach us. Therefore, our salvation lies in becoming so sensitive, or receptive, to the inner promptings of the Father's voice, that spiritual ideas unfolding within annul and shut out the aggressive mental suggestions of animal magnetism.

Simply wanting this communication to happen, or waiting passively for God to speak to us, is not enough. In Christian Science, an inner rapport with God begins with study. *We think and pray our way into the spiritual realm.* This metaphysical work begins with *reading Christian Science.* Even an experienced Scientist needs to read and ponder daily, the Bible, Mrs. Eddy's writings, and other important works on Christian Science. It may seem difficult at first to understand Christian Science, because there

86

seems to be so little within us to relate to divine Truth and Love. But we will never understand it unless we work at it through study and prayer. Daily we need to be alone with God, to read His Word, ponder the Truth, yearn to know what Christ Jesus knew that he could heal as he did. Then we listen from within, and so provide a receptive state of mind for God's thoughts to reach us.

As we study in this way, we introduce into consciousness ideas that are the opposite of the material view. When we read Christian Science — thinking, pondering, searching for the meaning of it — the Truth is active in consciousness, and we are receptive to the unfoldment of ideas that inspire and transform the inner self. As we think about the Truth, divine inspiration fills consciousness with illuminating thoughts from God. These spiritual ideas enable us to understand God. We become educated in divine realities. As the intelligence of divine Mind comes to light, we transcend the material view, and learn to think in the spiritual view.

This transcending experience is gradual. Because of a strongly developed material view, we identify with mortal beliefs easily. But through reading Christian Science, we develop a structure of intelligence that relates to divine ideas. This coming to light of spiritual understanding changes how we think.

To escape malpractice, we must completely renovate the inner self until we at last know God to be more real and powerful than animal magnetism. Such change begins with this daily study. If each day we gain one atom of spiritual enlightenment, one ray of truth, that we did not have the day before, this will gradually bring about our deliverance from evil.

Christian Science Treatment Essential

Through consecrated study, we begin to take control of our mind. Study is a free form of prayer, or treatment. As we read and meditate, listening for God's voice, His ideas unfold as our thoughts, and we establish in consciousness a spiritual foundation of Truth that protects the mind from malpractice. But this free-flowing, unstructured form of prayer, is not always enough to completely free consciousness of many hidden forms of animal magnetism, or defend the mind from malpractice. *For this, we need the treatment — the prayer of affirmation and denial. In the treatment, we take the initiative and argue FOR the allness of God, good, and AGAINST the power and reality of evil and matter.*

This mental work has the amazing effect of de-mesmerizing and spiritualizing consciousness, thus closing the mind to all malpractice. The treatment is a simple form of prayer designed to strengthen our conviction in the allness of God and the unreality of evil. *It is the most powerful form of intelligence on the earth today.* It will heal you and protect you from every claim of animal magnetism. It is the most effective means known for handling malpractice.

The simple act of denying the power and reality of evil, and affirming the allness of God, has a purifying and protecting effect on the mind not found in any other form of prayer. As the treatment is used against specific claims, it frees the mind of false beliefs embedded in consciousness, and makes it receptive to spiritual ideas. The Christ-consciousness becomes our consciousness, healing and protecting us from all evil.

Reference:

One Mind, Truth controls all. You are set free in the love of God, and you cannot make nor believe a lie. Truth declared is not reversed. It does appear and is manifest. No return of old beliefs. No M.A.M. to work through R.C., hypnotism, mesmerism, or theosophy, demonology, or old theology to hinder the work of the Cause of Christian Science. Divine Mind governs every hour and evil is powerless. (DC p 84)

WATCH - Evil is not power, not mind, and nobody has any power to accomplish evil of any sort (here stop and dwell on this argument till you realize this truth).

Then declare that Love is All and *in all*, in every thought, and all power is in Love. There is no other power. Evil is powerless; there is no evil.

Hypnotism, theosophy, and esoteric magic have no power to do evil, and cannot reverse Truth — but Life, Truth, Love *have reversed*, and they have destroyed all evil.

There are no false suggestions, lying arguments or hatred — these are illusions. They do not exist. I have no fear of them. *I am not controlled by them.* Divine Love is supreme and controls all I think, say, or do.

Pray daily twice at least to divine Love to give you success. Then realize for yourself that Love and Truth and action on your part (for Truth does not work for you unless you work) will give you the victory. Guard reversal. There is no law of hypnotism to reverse God's law. Truth is unchangeable and cannot be reversed. (DC p 47)

The simple prayer of affirmation and denial can be expanded upon in six carefully defined footsteps of treatment. This expanded version of the treatment makes the prayer more thorough and effective.

A brief example of the treatment is included here because it is the very essence of our work in Christian Science. It is the ultimate protection from malpractice. We read and study for the unfoldment of spiritual ideas. Then we use these ideas in the treatment. In doing so, we build up such a resistance to malpractice that it cannot reach us, or if it seems to, it cannot have a lasting effect on us.

We literally pray the treatment. In a silent, thoughtful frame of mind, alone with God, we affirm the Truth and deny all evil. This version of the treatment is focused on handling malpractice.

The six footsteps are as follows:

In the first footstep, begin by protecting the treatment. *Declare that this treatment is the Word of God and the truth about God and man.* In handling malpractice, we can declare that animal magnetism has no power or reality, and therefore this treatment cannot be invaded, annulled or reversed by ignorant, fraudulent or malicious malpractice.

In the second footstep, *affirm God through the synonyms.* This footstep focuses on God alone. It is designed to make you receptive to His ideas, aware of His spiritual nature. It is completely affirmative. There is no direct denial of malpractice in the second and third footsteps of treatment. Both are designed to help you understand the spiritual nature of God and man. Recall that it is an understanding of God, and not an analysis of evil, that delivers you from malpractice. A thorough affirmation of God in the first footstep, is the surest protection from hypnotic influence. The more we understand God, the less we are affected by malpractice.

You should begin this footstep with one of the definitions for God found in *Science and Health.* "God. The great I AM, the all-knowing, all-seeing, all-acting, all-wise, all-loving and eternal; Principle; Mind; Soul; Spirit; Life; Truth; Love; all substance; intelligence."

Here are listed the seven synonyms for God. To develop an understanding of God, you should research each synonym to find the attributes that define it best. This gives depth and meaning to these seven terms. It is through the seven synonyms that God becomes a living reality to you, the one Father-Mother, God.

The nature of God begins to unfold as you declare: *Life is being; Truth is reality; Love is power and relationship; Mind is intelligence, wisdom, understanding; Spirit is substance; Soul is identity; Principle is law.*

References:

> I have told you that evil has no power, yet I have told you to handle evil as though it had power. This is because of your place in growth spiritual. When the Allness of God is seen, the nothingness of evil is evident — hold to that.
> (DC p 197)

You will find a detailed explanation of the treatment in my works — *Christian Science Treatment: The Prayer that Heals* and *Scientific Prayer*. Also the booklet, *Animal Magnetism* is especially helpful in handling evil and malpractice in the treatment.

Next you can relate the synonyms to each other. In doing this you will find that each synonym gives a special insight into God, and together, they define the whole of God. In the second footstep, you can take the synonyms in whatever order you care to in relating them to each other.

You could choose to start with Life:

Life is being. Life is the ever-presence of God, creating and maintaining all things in perfect harmony. Man and the universe are eternal because Life is eternal — without beginning or end. Life is health, vitality, strength, freedom, boundless bliss. There is no opposing thought force in reality to obstruct the activity of Life and so Life is the effortless unfoldment of inexhaustible good.

Life is Truth. Life is ever-conscious of Truth, divine reality; therefore Life is immutable and immortal, because Truth is immutable and immortal. Life alone is real. Life and Truth maintain honesty, integrity, justice, and mercy in man and the universe untouched by any thought, word, or deed unlike God. The qualities of Life — joy, bliss, boundless freedom — represent true being, or reality.

Life is Love. All being is the expression of Love, for Life and Love are one, and only divine Love governs man's being. In the spiritual realm, the power of Love is the only presence and power, and Life is lived in the atmosphere of Love. Its ideas rejoice in the bliss of spiritual Life. To love is to live, for Love alone is Life.

Life is Mind. Life expresses intelligence, wisdom, understanding. All there is to be, God is; all there is to know, God knows; and so being is the expression of perfect intelligence. Each living thing is in reality an idea of Mind, and cannot think apart from Mind. It expresses the harmony and perfection of the Mind that creates and sustains it. Divine intelligence is one with Life, for both are immutable and immortal.

Life is Spirit. The forms that express Life originate in Spirit, substance, and are indestructible and perfect. Life is created and sustained by spiritual cause — intelligent, pure, loving, and good. Divine Life and spiritual cause and effect are one. Spirit is the only cause and creator, and this spiritual cause gives eternal life to all that it creates.

Life is Soul. Each idea is an individual expression of the inexhaustible resources of Soul, and is always one with the spiritual source that creates it. No thought or feeling unlike God can originate in Soul, or be part of the real universe and man.

Life is Principle. Life is governed by the laws of God. All being moves at one with God under the direction and control of the divine Principle, Love. The spiritual laws governing Life are loving, intelligent, and scientific. Life can never exist apart from Principle, for the divine laws of God govern life throughout eternity. In the whole of God's universe, there is not one harmful cause or effect.

For a thorough treatment, you should next relate the remaining synonyms to each other. For example, you can relate Truth to the other five synonyms.

Truth is reality. Truth reveals God as All-in-all; therefore man, made in God's likeness, is spiritual. Truth is eternal, immutable, immortal. Truth is expressed in the integrity, honesty, justice and mercy of God as He cares for man and the universe.

Truth is Love. It is a scientific fact that divine Love is the only power. God governs creation through divine Love, and the ultimate cause of all things real is a harmless, gentle, loving thought-force. Because Love is the reality of being, no foreign influence can enter the universe of Love.

Truth is Mind. The intelligence, wisdom, and understanding of divine Mind are Truth, void of a single negative element. Only the ideas of Mind express divine intelligence, or Truth. Truth alone reveals all that can be known about the spiritual realm.

Truth is Spirit. Truth reveals that all substance, all that comprises the universe and man, is spiritual in origin. All things are created, governed, and maintained by the divine thought-forces of Spirit — thought-forces that rule out any ungodlike influence. Reality is Spirit, divine substance, all good.

Truth is Soul. The divine identity of each idea reflects Truth alone. Soul's spontaneity, inspiration, and unfoldment, are always governed by Truth. Truth, or the Christ-consciousness, is true being or ego, and no other ego is present to interfere with God's handiwork. Truth, aglow with Love, is Soul, and imparts honesty, integrity, and goodness to all that Soul creates.

Truth is Principle. The spiritual, moral, and scientific laws of God are the foundation of reality. Reality is created and governed by Principle. All that is known as Truth must conform to the laws of God, and manifest the divine Principle, Love.

Next you can relate Love to the four remaining synonyms.

Love is power, relationship. Love is the presence of joy, happiness, peace, harmony, and perfection. It motivates all that God does. There is no stress, force, or conflict in God's universe, because all ideas unfold through the effortless action of Love. Love is the only power known to man, and no power other than God can influence or affect Love's creation and man. Love draws all ideas together in perfect harmony, and blesses creation with infinite good.

Love is Mind. Love is relationship, and the only intelligent relationship is a loving one. Therefore, all true relationships are bound together in pure affection, and can never be invaded by discord or conflict. They express divine intelligence, and unfold in the unified plan of the one Father-Mother God. The intelligence of Mind is permeated with Love, and the action of Mind is motivated by Love. The intelligence, wisdom, and understanding of Mind, and the gentleness, warmth, and caring of Love, are one.

Love is Spirit. Love is the substance of being. The spiritual forces creating and governing all things, are the all-powerful forces of Love. The spiritual dimension is divine Love, and so substance is harmless because Love is harmless. Spiritual being is controlled by infinite Love. Love is expressed in forms that are indestructible and eternal.

Love is Soul. Soul and Love are one; and each manifestation of Soul, embodying its own unique individuality, expresses Love, and can never affect another adversely. The intuitions of Soul unfold and ripen into fruition, for they are born in the atmosphere of Love and are nurtured by it.

Love is Principle. Love is a spiritual law, a divinely intelligent law. All cause is Love, the only power and presence in reality. Love enforces the laws of Principle with divine wisdom and understanding, and so unifies all things in perfect harmony. The divine Principle, Love is the only creator; therefore we live in a benign universe, a holy realm governed by divine laws, subject to Love's plan and purpose alone.

Next you can relate Mind to the remaining synonyms.

Mind is intelligence, wisdom, understanding. All that

can be known is included in divine intelligence, infallible wisdom, and spiritual understanding. The Science of being is made known to man through divine ideas that enable man to reflect the intelligence, wisdom, and understanding of Mind.

Mind is Spirit. Divine intelligence is true substance. Mind's ideas have the substance of Spirit, the substance of Life, Truth, and Love. They can never destroy or be destroyed. Mind, being spiritual, is intelligent, harmless, and good, giving to man divine intelligence, wisdom, and understanding.

Mind is Soul. The intelligent activity of Mind is expressed in spiritual ideas, which unfold the purity of Soul. The ideas of Mind fill the ego or identity of man, and these ideas are not only intelligent, wise and good, but they are harmless.

Mind is Principle. The ideas of Mind operate in accord with Principle and its laws. In the whole of creation, there is one Principle, Mind, one supreme, intelligent cause expressing itself in one perfect effect.

Next you can relate Spirit to Soul and Principle.

Spirit is substance. Underlying all things is the spiritual dimension wherein rests the cause and continuity of all things real. Only as man and the universe are interpreted spiritually, can they be understood.

Spirit is Soul. The substance of the universe and man is manifested in infinite individuality. The spiritual ideas of Mind are given identity through Soul. All ego, or identity, is filled with spiritual understanding, true knowledge, perfect intelligence, pure love — individualized as true substance or being. Such spiritual identity is incapable of thoughts that would harm another.

Spirit is Principle. The Principle, or primal cause of all things real, is Spirit. The substance of the universe is indestructible, harmless, good, because it is created and governed by the divine Principle, Love. Spiritual laws govern all that God creates in perfect unity — one divine cause and effect, perfect God, perfect man, perfect universe.

Now relate Soul to Principle.

Soul is identity, individuality, ego; Principle is law, order, plan, unity.

Soul is Principle. True identity is governed by the laws of Principle, and is obedient to them. Every idea in Mind is subject to the divine Principle, Love, which creates and governs all individuality. The laws of Principle enhance the ideas of Soul by giving them an intelligent and stable foundation. The Soul-senses are cognizant only of the spiritual realm. In this realm the unfoldment of all identity is orderly, planned, and directed by the divine Principle, Love, and cannot be invaded by any ungodlike element.

Reference:

The divine law of Life, Truth and Love is a law of instant and complete expulsion and elimination of all poisons and impurities from the system. Why? Because the floodtides of divine Life, Truth and Love are pouring and surging through consciousness, uplifting, purifying, nourishing, healing, elevating, sustaining and energizing mankind. (DC p 227)

The purpose of this work is not to rehearse statements of truth, but to become accustomed to thinking in spiritual ideas, so that there unfolds a mental atmosphere through which God can reach you.

As you meditate each day on the synonyms and their relation to each other, you will begin to sense the presence of a new dimension all around you. And it will be a thinking, intelligent presence creating and governing all things, including all that relates to your own life. The more distinct and real this presence is to you, the greater your protection from malpractice, for evil thoughts cannot enter a consciousness aware of the presence of the spiritual dimension.

In the third footstep of treatment, you can *relate man to the synonyms.*

Man expresses Life, being. Man exists as a complete and perfect idea of God. Perfection is natural to his being. Since man is the effect of the one divine cause, nothing can sever his relationship with his Father-Mother God. His origin being indestructible, man is indestructible. Man is never outside of divine Life. He expresses Life, and possesses every good thing. Man is deathless, eternal. His real being is held intact forever in the one Life. Only what God is doing for man ever comes into his experience. As God's reflection, he expresses health, vitality, activity. His oneness with God protects him from all that is unlike God.

Man knows Truth as reality. Truth is the intelligence of man. Man reflects divine Science, and Truth alone is real to him. Man thinks in Truth effortlessly, for it is the whole of his being. He knows the Truth, and he knows he knows it. Truth, or Science, is practical and rational to him. Truth is all to him, and there is nothing beyond it, and so he is beyond the reach of all ungodly thoughts. With a consciousness filled with Truth, nothing unlike Truth can enter his being.

In the realm of Love, man is the beloved. He is secure in divine Love. As God's idea, he is as safe as God Himself. Nothing can cloud over his sense of oneness, or unity, with the divine Principle, Love. As the child of God, man expresses the qualities of Love — affection, kindness, tenderness, gentleness, patience, compassion, forgiveness, humility, and gratitude. These qualities enable man to reflect the power of Love. In the whole of man's being there is not one harmful element. He is immune to all negative influence, because he knows and expresses only the purity of divine Love.

Man dwells in the eternal Mind. As the reflection of Mind, man does not believe; *he knows.* Mind knows all things, and man's reflection of this knowing is perfect, complete. Being one with Mind, man receives only the mental impressions of God, and no other mind can reach him. He is the work of God, obedient to Mind alone. In humility, he discerns and reflects the spiritual ideas that unfold as his very being. These ideas are manifested as intelligence, wisdom, and understanding. They are used by man in all that he thinks, and says, and does.

The substance of man's existence is Spirit, the only cause and creator. Spiritual existence is good, healthful, holy. Man understands the nature of the spiritual dimension. He knows he is never outside of its divine atmosphere. Man lives in spiritual substance, for spiritual qualities and ideas are the substance of his being. His senses can discern only the spiritual nature of all things, for he lives in Spirit.

Man expresses Soul. Man's ego, or identity, is wholly spiritual. His true individuality is "hid with Christ in God." Divine ideas unfold and maintain his perfection, thus shutting out any other mental influence. His ego is creative, loving, gracious, inspired, beautiful, Godlike, poised in the realm of Love. He is the expression of the pure and sinless qualities of Soul, and lives in the uncontaminated realm of Mind. He is complete in Soul.

The laws of Principle govern man. These laws give unity and plan to his life. He reflects the law of Love, the law of Life, the law of intelligence, the law of abundance. God creates a universe that blesses man, and he lives in a totally benign environment, both mental and physical. His life unfolds according to the laws of Principle. Obedient to these laws, man is blessed with dominion over all the earth.

When you have related man to the synonyms, identify with these prayerful affirmations by declaring, "I am that man!" It is essential that you realize that you really are spiritual man — made in God's likeness. The purpose of this work is to understand that, here and now, these affirmations are true about you. Not only is God, Mind, present, maintaining the spiritual universe and man, but you are spiritual man living in the spiritual universe. Your work is meant to bring to light the one Mind and your oneness with it.

The second and third footsteps are the affirmative part of treatment. You are trying to realize the Truth, and so replace the material view with the spiritual. The statements in this portion of the work should be positive declarations of Truth. It does require practice to discipline yourself to think in spiritual realities alone; but if you persist in this work, it becomes easier to think in the true view than the false one.

Reference:

Mortal mind cannot mesmerize me into a belief that I can have any disease so-called, for I am an idea of God, perfect, harmonious, and eternal, and cannot be mesmerized. It cannot say to me, 'It is yourself that has a disease, etc.', for I am perfect, and it cannot make me think that I am it. (DC p 70)

No subtlety or sophistry of evil can blind or paralyze my human capacity to apprehend and love good. (DC p 177)

Electricity is the counterfeit of the descent of the Holy Ghost. (DC p 208)

Electricity is the thought essence which forms the link between what is matter and mortal mind. God, the divine Mind, self-existent, self-perpetuating, and self-energizing, is the great reservoir, or dynamo, and the thoughts which flow from such fountains, constituting a complete expression of that infinite Mind, Spirit, are thus shown to be inseparably linked with the Principle of Life and action and to be the manifestation of spiritual force or power. (DC p 148)

In the fourth footstep, *deny animal magnetism and malpractice.* In the second and third footsteps, the declarations of Truth are made in a positive, receptive state of mind; but the denial of evil and matter is made with strong, even vehement, rejections of evil. You are working to de-mesmerize consciousness, to free it of every claim of evil, and to protect it from hypnotic influence.

If you fight daily against the belief in evil and matter, you will experience definite spiritual progress, and mental freedom from the malpractice around you.

This footstep begins with *the denial of matter through the synonyms.* Declare that there is no life in matter, and no matter in Life; no truth in matter, and no matter in Truth; no love or power in matter, and no matter in Love; no mind in matter, and no matter in Mind; no spirit in matter, and no matter in Spirit; no soul in matter, and no matter in Soul; no law or principle in matter, and no matter in divine Principle and its laws.

Think carefully about these statements, for they begin to breakdown the belief in matter. Material law, cause and effect, should also be vigorously denied.

Next *declare against the false traits of mortal mind.* Mortal elements in consciousness are the means through which malpractice reaches you — the many various claims of fear, hatred, and self-will that seem to be a mortal personality. Deny all subtle forms of sin, such as criticism, self-righteousness, self-justi-fication, self-love, anger, impatience, irritation, disappointment, guilt,

100

self-condemnation. Determine the false traits that are most predominant in yourself, and with the truth, reject these self-hypnotic states that cause you to malpractice on yourself, and allow the malpractice of others to affect you.

In handling matter and mortal mind, you handle the *effects* of animal magnetism. But you need to go one step further and handle the *cause* itself. In this you must be strong, aggressive, even vehement, in your denial. Force animal magnetism out of consciousness. Fight with it! Look through every kind of mortal belief, and see behind it, evil arguing hypnotic suggestions to you. Then face evil and declare: There is no power or energy in you. There is no Principle or law in you; no Soul or ego in you; no Spirit or substance in you; no Mind or intelligence or wisdom in you; no Love or power in you; no Truth or reality in you; no Life or being in you. Having denied animal magnetism, you should then address it directly, and vehemently demand, You are to stop arguing to me! You are to stop mesmerizing or controlling me! You are to loose me and let me go!

Stand up to evil! Back it down again and again. Reject its hypnotic suggestions. Refuse to think anything evil or discordant. You must struggle with each hypnotic illusion until you feel it fade out of consciousness.

Find your own way of resisting evil, but do it! Don't neglect this part of treatment. If your affirmations of Truth have been strong and inspiring, this vehement denial of evil will so challenge it, that it will weaken, dissolve, and finally disappear from consciousness. *It is the fear of evil that gives it the illusion of having power over you. When you can stand absolutely unintimidated by it, you then have dominion over it, and it collapses into nothingness. It ceases to be part of your consciousness and can no longer appear as a seeming reality in your experience.*

Take control of your mind and resist animal magnetism with the absolute conviction that good destroys evil. Each time you declare the simple facts — that evil has no law, energy, intelligence or power, no reality or substance, that there is no Mind in evil and no God in it — you are exercising your dominion over it.

Having brought the truth to bear on evil, you can now *deny malpractice with power and authority.* See it as evil's hatred of the Christ-consciousness. It is a total violation of the law of Love. See it as a common form of animal magnetism that claims to control the mind. Is there Love in malpractice? Does it give Life? Is it divinely intelligent? Is it principled? Is there any Truth in malpractice? Is it part of Soul, or one's divine identity? No! Then it does not originate in God.

Reference:

Animal magnetism cannot make me restless or dissatisfied; cannot suggest to me any doubt of the absolute Truth of Christian Science; cannot make a law that I cannot heal; that I cannot succeed; that I will not heal my patients; cannot frighten me or prevent me from healing others; cannot darken my thought, nor dim my spiritual perception; cannot produce or bring back a belief with an argument or poison of any kind (name). (DC p 273)

The moment you are pleasant with or in error, that moment you can do nothing with it. There must be *authority*. It is not seeking but striving that enables us to conquer.
(DC p 18)

Animal magnetism is powerless — but you must declare against it as though it had ALL POWER. (DC p 197)

Therefore you can argue that it is no part of man. In the whole of God's universe there is not one act of malpractice — not one! Think about that. Therefore know that you cannot be mesmerized by the hypnotic influence of animal magnetism. You cannot be made to fear malpractice, for it cannot mesmerize you. Evil has no power to affect your Christ-consciousness, for you are hidden in the "secret place," one with God. It is important to deal directly with this belief and handle it in treatment until you are free of it.

This denial of malpractice can be changed to apply to any specific form of malpractice that you seem to be meeting. Such strong arguments, used at times when malpractice is especially aggressive, can provide protection and prevent malpractice from causing serious problems. But this protection is most effective when you have been working each day with the general treatment, for only then will your declarations be accompanied with an understanding that makes them effective.

It is also good in this fourth footstep to deny specific forms of malpractice that claim to work against Christian Science. Declare that there is no power or reality in Roman Catholicism, occultism, Orientalism, witchcraft, Satanism, astrology, numerology, psychology, etc. There is no 'ism' or 'ology' named or unnamed, known or unknown, that can intrude upon the Christ-consciousness within.

References:

Theology, spiritualism, theosophy, psychology, occultism, false philosophy, false science, mesmerism, hypnotism, oriental witchcraft, black art, black magic, astrology, palmistry, demonology, diabolism, thought transference, are things to be handled occasionally; they are arguments which tend to perpetuate evil and death in the name of good. (DC p 90)

There is no hypnotism or mesmerism for R.C. to operate through, no activity, energy, will, law, mind or minds to give operation to hypnotism or mesmerism. Every idea of Truth acts according to its own law. Try to realize the allness and presence of God. You are His image and likeness. There is no lack of resuscitation. God's law is the law of resuscitation. There is no inaction in Mind, no lethargy, no insanity, no stagnation, no hypnotism, no evil; nor can any of its claims subtly take possession of the so-called mortal mind, for Mind is God, ever conscious, ever acting, all motion. There is no electricity to poison the nerve centers. There is no deterioration, no disintegration; no form of woman to waste away; no destruction, no cohesion. (DC p 67)

While it is absolutely essential to handle animal magnetism, the fourth footstep should not, as a rule, overshadow the rest of the treatment. The denial of evil must be done; but it is the realization of Truth that heals.

Whatever the discord or error may seem to be, its origin is in evil's hatred of the Christ-consciousness, its sadism, its mental and physical cruelty. Fight it out with the cause — animal magnetism. When you have been successful in this battle and have destroyed the hypnotic hold of malpractice, you will know it, for you are mentally free of the suggestion and healing follows.

You must take the time to do a thorough job of the denial portion of treatment for this will free you of the effects of malpractice. When you avoid handling animal magnetism and confine the work to positive declarations of Truth alone, the work may fail to bring about healing results.

There are occasions when almost the entire treatment should be given to the denial of animal magnetism. As a rule, the affirmation of Truth is so important that it should have the major portion of a treatment, but there are exceptions to this. When error is stirred, or aggressive, or coming to the surface of consciousness to be destroyed, then you need to recognize this, and devote sufficient work to destroying it. The approach to treating malpractice changes with each claim. If you feel the need to devote time to the denial of evil, and it is proving effective, then stay with it.

There may be times when malpractice is so aggressive that you must begin your treatment with the vehement denial of evil, and keep denying it until you are in control of your thoughts. Then, to complete the work, follow your denial with the affirmation of the truth about God and man until you sense that the danger is past.

Sometimes the malpractice will be so unrelenting that you have to wear it down day after day with a constant denial of its seeming reality. This repetitious denial of evil counteracts its hypnotic suggestions, and eventually breaks it down and destroys it. *You can do this!* Do make full use of the healing power of the treatment in a thorough denial of animal magnetism.

In the fifth footstep, *affirm the oneness of God and man.* Declare that God is the one Father-Mother, and man is His child. God and man are one as cause and effect. In reality, man is under the influence of Mind alone, and one with divine intelligence.

Work with the fifth footstep until you are uplifted and inspired with a spiritual sense of being. This footstep lifts thought out of the negative handling of animal magnetism, and finishes the treatment on a spiritual note.

Then again, in the sixth footstep, *protect your work* by knowing that this treatment is the Word of God, and cannot be annulled or reversed. It will not return void, but must accomplish its purpose.

You need to concentrate on every declaration of truth and denial of error you make. Think about the work you are doing. Focus hard on the ideas you are trying to realize. As you do, you break down the resistance of animal magnetism to your work, and your treatment is then a constant source of joy and inspiration.

The treatment is a *prayer of action*. Equipped with the fact that God is All and evil is unreal, you take the initiative and fight all hypnotic suggestions with the truth until you clear your mind. This metaphysical work is entirely subjective. It is an inner struggle between good and evil. The fight takes place on your own mental terrain. It is an unforgettable moment when you take the offensive, and fight against a claim of animal magnetism with the truth, and find that your treatment does indeed destroy the claim! The aggressive mental suggestion that seemed so real and powerful gives way, and you are free of it. Thus, study and treatment enables you to face malpractice and vigorously, adamantly deny its power and reality, and continue the battle until you gain dominion over it.

Always remember, malpractice has no power over God. It cannot influence God against you. Malicious mental malpractice cannot separate you from the Father's care. It cannot turn God against you, or annul and reverse the good that unfolds through your prayerful work. It cannot enter the Christ-consciousness — your true selfhood. It can only influence its own false mentality. It can only mesmerize, control and destroy itself. Its assumed power claims to exist solely within the Adam-dream. Once you realize this, you rise above a fear of it. As you conquer your fear of what others are thinking, you are divinely protected from malpractice.

References:

There is no hypnotism or mesmerism for R.C. [Roman Catholicism] to operate through, no activity, energy, will, law, mind or minds to give operation to hypnotism or mesmerism. Every idea of Truth acts according to its own law. Try to realize the allness and presence of God. You are His image and likeness. There is no lack of resuscitation. God's law is the law of resuscitation. There is no inaction in Mind, no lethargy, no insanity, no stagnation, no hypnotism, no evil; nor can any of its claims subtly take

106

possession of the so-called mortal mind, for Mind is God, ever conscious, ever acting, all motion. There is no electricity to poison the nerve centers. There is no deterioration, no disintegration; no form of woman to waste away; no destruction, no cohesion. (DC p 67)

There is no animal, vegetable or mineral kingdom, there is no poisonous thought or mind. There can be no inflammation from fear, hate, lust or poison, through mental malpractice or mental malpractitioners. There is no mind to transfer or be transferred, telegraphed or transmitted, and no man or woman to operate those claims. (DC p 284)

Keeping Malpractice Impersonal

In working out claims caused by our own mortal beliefs, we have only our own thinking to correct. But in the handling of malpractice, we must consider the thoughts and feelings of another. In obedience to the law of Love, we must be concerned over his welfare, regardless of the fact that he is ignorantly or intentionally malpracticing on us.

It is of utmost importance that *we do not take malpractice personally!* When we are the victim of malpractice, our first reaction is usually one of hurt feelings, anger, revenge, fear, hate, self-justification, self-righteousness, etc., which are directed towards the malpractitioner. When we react with such personal feelings, we are on the same mental plane that he is on. If we malpractice on him, we have no defense against his malpractice.

It is not his thoughts, but his emotions that make the malpractice so destructive. When we retaliate with the same emotions, we suffer from both his thoughts and our own. If we use the treatment as a tool for personally attacking and punishing another, we can do great harm to him, and it will destroy our own spirituality. In doing so, we are engaged in a negative treatment, or a denial of another's Christ-consciousness. This is not permitted in Christian Science.

We must go about the handling of malpractice carefully, lovingly, scientifically. Since malpractice is not person, we begin by *separating malicious animal magnetism from the person and handling the error alone.* We do this by being loving and forgiving towards the individual, while strongly denying malpractice as evil's hatred of the Christ-consciousness.

There have been countless instances when a difficult situation involving malpractice have been resolved when the Scientist has risen above personal sense, and has so annulled the mental attack in his own consciousness that he has only Christly love and forgiveness for the other person.

There have also been instances when the unscientific handling of the mind of another have had disastrous results for both parties.

We must, above all else, strive never to harm another through our own mental work in Christian Science. A mind and heart that is loving cannot harm another whatever the other person may be thinking about him. Hatred, criticism, condemnation, etc. are instant forms of malpractice, and can do another great damage. But a heart filled with Christly love cannot afflict another while denying malpractice.

If we are inclined to react to malpractice, we need to determine what elements within our own consciousness cause us to take the malpractice personally. Then we can purify consciousness until we rise above personal sense, separate malpractice from the person and forgive him, while handling the malpractice as impersonal evil. It is essential that we learn to do this if we are to be beyond the reach of malpractice.

As we study and pray in Science, we discern an unrelenting war between good and evil in the mental realm. We learn that evil is not passive and inert; it is aggressive. When it cannot handle us from within, it tries to stop our spiritual progress by attacking us through the malpractice of others. Malicious malpractice is not an act of personal hatred; it is animal magnetism using another's mind to attack us, pull us down into the dark, chaotic world of personal sense, and keep us there.

So long as animal magnetism can keep us fighting with one another, the Christly love of our true selfhood cannot come to light. But when we get beyond personal sense, and see every conflict as animal magnetism attacking the Christ, trying to cause conflict and hostility, we can then forgive the person while dealing with the malpractice. If we learn to do this, our work in Christian Science will bring the day when we can face every type of malpractice and remain totally unmoved by it, knowing it is powerless and unreal. Then we will be able to deal with it scientifically, and realize an easy victory over it.

References:

To run before a lie is to accept its terms. This works like running before the enemy in battle. You will be followed, pursued, till you face about, *trust* in *God* and stand on *Spirit* denying and facing and fighting all claims of matter and mortal mind both one, and you have grown to be honored by God with entrance into this department of learning. (DC p 111)

Since malicious animal magnetism knows all the arguments of Christian Science it is necessary to declare that no argument of mental malpractice can make null and void, antidote or reverse, any statement of Christian Science that you make. (DC p 277)

Animal magnetism, hypnotism, etc., are disarmed by the practitioner who excludes from his own consciousness, and that of his patients, all sense of the realism of any other cause or effect save that which cometh from God. And he should teach his students to defend themselves from all evil, and to heal the sick, by recognizing the supremacy and allness of good. This epitomizes what heals all manner of sickness and disease, moral or physical. (My 364)

Mental malpractice cannot reverse my declarations, cannot touch my conscious or unconscious thought, for there are not minds many. There is only one Mind, divine Mind. (DC p 49)

'Let God do it.' Do not allow that thought of the person who has tried to injure you enter your thought! Destroy in your thought all envy, jealousy, and hate, and other errors, and the light will shine in your thought and heal you and very likely the other person also. (DC p 125)

Determining a Source

Animal magnetism always has an agent, a mind it is using to spread its lies. Although we must impersonalize malpractice, it is also helpful to know the source of the malpractice — the avenue through which animal magnetism is claiming to operate. If we feel a claim is caused by malpractice, and we cannot detect the source of it, we can pray to be shown the answer. Seeking divine guidance will often reveal the source. Once we have determined the source, this may be enough to end the attack, for when animal magnetism is uncovered, its power diminishes, and it fades away. Also, knowing the source, we have more direction, control and assurance in handling it.

If we deny the power and reality of malpractice coming from a certain person, and feel a change in the physical or mental condition, we have usually been correct in determining the source, and the claim will lift as we continue to work. In detecting the source, we can handle it scientifically by separating the malpractice from persons, and gradually gaining dominion over the hypnotic influence in our own consciousness.

The most foolproof way of protecting our mind is to eliminate personal sense that reacts to malpractice. When we can stand absolutely unintimidated, unmoved, undisturbed by these attacks, then they usually have little or no effect on us, and are even removed from our experience.

If a belief, or physical claim, seems to be met only to return, or if we have one overwhelming problem after another, such experiences are usually due to malpractice. Moreover, a practitioner cannot always meet a claim for a patient if malpractice is the cause. He can counteract the malpractice for the patient, and so long as he is handling it, his metaphysical work will block out the malpractice for the patient. But when he stops working, the malpractice will usually begin again, and the claim will return. For this reason, we must learn to do our own metaphysical work in meeting malpractice.

References:

Do not address the individuality, but talk to yourself as you would if you had a belief. Say to yourself, such an individual cannot deceive me as to himself and others; has no power over me. I don't believe his lies, and cannot be made to believe them. He cannot frighten me. Evil is powerless, and God is All, etc. Argue that you cannot be made to believe that you cannot protect yourself from his influence.
(DC p 135)

Neither animal magnetism nor hypnotism enters into the practice of Christian Science, in which truth cannot be reversed, but the reverse of error is true. (S&H 442)

No Shortcuts to this Work

We must learn how to detect and destroy malpractice scientifically, if we are to be protected from it. Today, as in the past, some Christian Scientists simply refuse to acknowledge that it needs to be handled. They insist that it is nothing. Those who take only an affirmative approach, are sometimes called 'Absolutists,' for they hold to the absolute teachings of Christian Science alone and refuse to acknowledge the need to handle evil. A mind dwelling in absolute Science, unwilling to face and handle malpractice, actually has very little defense against it.

There are also those who believe that a deep abiding faith in Christian Science, daily study of the Lesson-Sermons, and an unswerving devotion to the Church, are adequate protection.

Then some Scientists become so obsessed with diagnosing animal magnetism and malpractice that they stagnate at this level, usually satisfied with the study of animal magnetism, almost as though this were the purpose of Christian Science — detecting animal magnetism and malpractice in others. They may tend to blame all their problems on malpractice, and make others a scapegoat for their own lack of demonstration.

Still another type believes that a warm, gentle, forgiving thought is protection enough from all evil. A beautiful sense of love, whereby we do not hold any unkind thoughts towards others, is a great step beyond personal sense filled with negative emotions. But spiritual love must include a large degree of spiritual wisdom and insight into the workings of evil, in order for the mind to be properly protected. Otherwise, the loving thought is totally undefended against the malice that attacks human goodness, and so it becomes a target for malpractice. One cannot rest in a loving sense of others, but he must become knowledgeable about the nature of evil and how it operates.

CHRISTIAN SCIENCE: THE ONE TRUE DEFENSE

These are mistaken efforts to handle malpractice in a simple, easy way, avoiding the hard work of demonstrating a true defense. Such naive approach to malpractice could account for the seeming incurable claims and untimely deaths of those who are faithfully serving the Christian Science Cause. If we are going to progress in Christian Science, we must early in our work recognize the absolute necessity to handle malpractice.

Reference:

Certain individuals entertain the notion that Christian Science Mind-healing should be two-sided, and only denounce error in general, — saying nothing, in particular, of error that is damning men. They are sticklers for a false, convenient peace, straining at gnats and swallowing camels. The unseen wrong to individuals and society they are too cowardly, too ignorant, or too wicked to uncover, and excuse themselves by denying that this evil exists. This mistaken way, of hiding sin in order to maintain harmony, has licensed evil, allowing it first to smoulder, and then break out in devouring flames. All that error asks is to be let alone; even as in Jesus' time the unclean spirits cried out, "Let us alone; what have we to do with thee?" (My 211)

The Law of Separation

As we progress in Science, we become increasingly aware of the destructive effects of malpractice, and we learn to have great respect for it. Far from dismissing it as 'nothing,' we learn that it is a mental force in human experience that inflicts cruel and unrelieved suffering on humanity. We must learn to handle it.

We also learn that there are times when malpractice is so strong, so long lasting, so malicious and aggressive, that we are, at this time, unable to rise above it in Christian Science. Some Scientists find this fact shocking — that there are attacks of such hypnotic force and duration that they are beyond our present ability to overcome. But this is true, and it needs to be brought out so that, should the reader ever encounter this challenge, he will understand what he is up against.

There are four general categories of such malpractice:

> 1. *Malpractice that is so violent, malicious and aggressive that it amounts to extreme mental cruelty.*
> 2. *The collective malpractice of many minds circulating malicious gossip, accusations, or slander that amounts to mental assassination.*
> 3. *Unrelenting malicious malpractice that the victim must endure day in and day out without relief.*
> 4. *The malicious malpractice of those who practice secret hypnotism.*

What if we find ourselves faced with malpractice so aggressive that it is a threat to our health, even our life, and we cannot meet it? The spiritual answer to this challenge is in what could be termed *the law of separation.*

We often hear it said in Christian Science that we must stay with an inharmonious relationship, or situation, until we heal it. But this is not a realistic approach to relationships involving such forms of malicious malpractice as those listed above.

What are we to do if we have handled malpractice to the best of our ability, and there is no improvement in the situation, no let up in the malpractice? Have we failed in our effort to handle the problem? Not necessarily. There are times when the malpractice we meet from another causes such intense emotional and mental distress, such physical pain and suffering, that remaining within the range of such malpractice is neither a wise nor intelligent decision, and so the law of separation operates to save us from the evil that threatens to overcome us. Contrary to the belief that a Scientist must remain in every situation, and assume the responsibility of demonstrating harmony for *all* involved, he can pray to be shown how to escape the malpractice and thus save himself.

Certainly we should make every effort to demonstrate harmony in all areas of our life; but if there is no response to our work, this law provides an escape and refuge from extreme suffering experiences that defy healing.

In this human experience, there are mentalities sunken so deep into materialism, sensualism, and selfishness, that they malpractice constantly. They seem so void of the Christ-consciousness that our metaphysical work has no effect on them — unless to antagonize them. They usually consider the gentle, loving, giving person as one to be patronized, scorned, used, and abused.

As a rule, those who are of this nature are hardened in their ways, and have no intention of changing; and so it is not required of us to remain within the range of such malicious malpractice, for it will retard our progress, and even reverse our healing work, while being of no benefit to the others.

Chronic mental and emotional illness, disease, even death, can be due to unrelieved mental malpractice coming from a relationship in which there is intense hatred towards the victim.

But we learn in Christian Science that *we do not have to endure hateful relationships.* By leading us to believe we cannot leave a situation without first healing it, animal magnetism would permanently bind us to such relationships, and so succeed in obstructing our spiritual progress. If we find ourselves the victim of malicious malpractice that is insurmountable, we have a way out by yielding to the law of separation. This law acts to separate the progressive Scientist from abusive malpractice that is never going to yield to his healing efforts.

MENTAL MALPRACTICE

The law of unity draws to us those with whom we can relate harmoniously. The law of separation acts to separate us from those who are incompatible, difficult, hateful, abusive, who malpractice unmercifully on others. Unless we understand this law, we are inclined to resist its operation.

If our metaphysical work produces distance, rather than closeness, in a difficult relationship, or causes a relationship to dissolve, thus freeing us of it, we may mistake what is happening, and assume we are not working correctly. We need to realize that if our work fails to bring about harmony and unity, then quite often a parting of the ways *is* the demonstration, leaving *is* the healing, separation *is* the answer.

As we study and live Christian Science, our thoughts become increasingly spiritualized. This naturally separates us from the materialistic mentality that absorbs the worldly scene and lives by its standards. There is always a great distance between the materially darkened mind and the spiritually enlightened one — a gulf that increases as they move in opposite directions. Sometimes this difference between them inflames the animal magnetism in the one, and produces a chemicalization that intensifies the malpractice. But our prayerful work should bring into operation the law of separation, which acts to free ourselves and the other person from the conflict that is inevitable when one is progressing spiritually, and the other is determined to remain in a material state of mind.

It is important to understand this law, for only then do we see that there is a spiritual answer to dealing with a material, sensual mortal who has no conscience about malpracticing on others. With such individuals, a happy association is not likely to come about. Thus the law of separation operates to bring about the highest degree of harmony possible under the circumstances. It does so by separating the material and spiritual mentalities.

It is neither just nor merciful for the devoted Scientist to suffer indefinitely for the sins of another. It is not the design of a

116

loving Father-Mother God to impose an impossible task on us by requiring that we stay with a malpracticing mentality until we heal it — when such a demonstration is not presently possible.

Throughout her writings, Mrs. Eddy separates good and evil, the spiritual and the material, truth and error, "which neither dwell together nor assimilate." She also writes in *Science and Health*, "Mortal belief (the material sense of life) and immortal Truth (the spiritual sense) are the tares and wheat, which are not united by progress, but separated." Although her statements are used to describe the error and truth within our own consciousness, she also recognized that those who are striving to understand Christian Science would eventually rise above worldly relationships into a purer mental atmosphere. For those doing so, she writes in *Science and Health*, "Wisdom will ultimately put asunder what she hath not joined together." She also writes in *Miscellaneous Writings*, "Science lifts humanity higher in the scale of harmony, and must ultimately break all bonds that hinder progress."

We see, then, that if we encounter malpractice that is obstinate, abusive, and threatening, we have a way out — we can let God separate us from the malpractitioner. When we are willing to let the law of separation operate, when we let go of all human outlining, all self-will, all emotional yearning and involvement, and pray earnestly for God's will to be done, we open the way for the Father to work out the problem.

The law of separation operates in all areas of our life, lifting us above the miasma of mortal mind, freeing us of relationships we have outgrown, loosening us from the pull of human desires, pleasures and pastimes, and giving us a refuge and escape from malicious malpractice so intense and so unrelenting that we cannot counteract it with our present understanding of Science. As we understand this law, we learn to yield to it and let the relationship dissolve.

117

If you are willing to do this, and the way does not open to leave, then it is likely you are still holding in consciousness some mortal emotion that keeps you bound to the relationship — a false sense of responsibility, curiosity, dislike, fear, physical or sensual or personal attraction, sadness over his problems, a sense of dependency, a hope he will change, etc. Even the desire to help him and save him from the inevitable suffering that malpractice brings on — this alone will keep the law of separation from operating to help us escape such an inharmonious relationship.

If we seem to be meeting intense malicious malpractice, and our work is not freeing us of its harmful effects, and we cannot leave, then we have spiritual lessons to learn from it. If we find ourselves in this situation, there is one thing more we can do in Christian Science — *we can out last it*. However long and tenacious the malpractice, it is temporary. It is never part of our real being, and so, instead of making a reality of it, we can see it as false suggestion that must sooner or later yield to our metaphysical work and disappear. We can hold to the truth and 'tough it out,' never doubting God's ability to bring us through the ordeal.

If we do this, praying to learn from the experience all that it has to teach us, our prayers will be answered. It is likely we will learn very advanced lessons in Christian Science from our willingness to endure the experience as long as there is something to learn from it, for when we have learned from the experience all it has to teach us, we will be lifted out of it. Such a victory over malicious malpractice brings great spiritual growth.

References:

There is nothing about me that attracts, corresponds with, or responds to, any form of error or evil. In proportion to your realization of this are you immune to the mesmeric and hypnotic influences of A.M. (DC p 79)

WATCH - Hold on and persist for good, because there never is a hopeless situation. When error meets with resistance, it begins to be scattered. Where a situation seems unbearable, it is because error is letting go. (DC p 40)

Summary

Outside of Christian Science, malpractice seems ominous, an ever-present threat to our entire existence. But once we learn to handle it in Christian Science, its seeming reality and power collapses. We realize that the only power it can exercise over us, is what we allow it to have. As we rise above personal sense, malpractice can have no lasting effect on us. The fear of it is gone, and it fades into oblivion.

The secret to healing and protecting the mind lies in understanding God — not analyzing evil. We are protected to the degree that we think and live in the atmosphere of divine intelligence and love. Evil seems to mesmerize us and produce mental and physical suffering, because it finds mortal elements within our own consciousness that respond to its influence. So long as we are preoccupied with evil — analyzing it, observing it, fearing it, disapproving of it, or making a reality of it in any way — we are vulnerable to its influence. There are times when it is necessary to know what evil seems to be doing, and to discern how it is claiming to operate; but this is the least of our work in Christian Science. Our major goal is to develop such a clear understanding of God that evil becomes unreal to us. This spiritualization of thought comes through study and treatment. Daily metaphysical work spiritualizes consciousness to such a degree that we can discern the difference between the angel thoughts of God and the evil influence of animal magnetism. In time we learn to dwell in the angel thoughts alone, and live beyond the reach of animal magnetism.

Chapter VII

CONCLUSION

You will find as you advance in your study of Christian Science, that a knowledge of malpractice and how it operates is absolutely essential. At first, the need to deal with it may be overwhelming; but as the ideas presented here settle into consciousness, you will find yourself intuitively discerning it when it takes place in your personal life, and you will become adept at refusing to accept it into your consciousness.

You may at times encounter the more aggressive forms of collective, malicious malpractice. Often Christian Scientists do not understand why they "have so much to meet." But when you recognize these challenges as the antichrist attacking the Christ-consciousness and attempting to stop your work, you are able to impersonalize the attack, and rise above it.

The most malicious forms of malpractice coming from trained hypnotists are something you will seldom, if ever, encounter. Should you do so, God will give you the wisdom and strength to meet them.

While you must know about malpractice, it is also important that you keep it in proper perspective in your overall study of Christian Science. The real purpose of study and prayer is to understand God. Spiritual progress does not come in knowing about evil, but in knowing about God. To understand God brings to light the spiritual dimension. The purpose of Christian Science is to make this hidden dimension — this kingdom of God — a present reality.

To do this, we must spiritualize consciousness through the study of Christian Science, and the prayer of affirmation and denial. Through study and prayer, we work to understand God and develop the spiritual view, while vigorously denying the power and reality of evil and matter. This mighty effort changes how we think. We begin adding a spiritual dimension to our view of God, man and the universe. This metaphysical work reveals to us the healing and transforming power latent in this unseen dimension.

Success in this work is the ultimate protection from every kind of malpractice. As we know God, we know man and ourselves as God's image and likeness. At the same time, we lose the mortal traits and material view that allow malpractice to handle us. Since there must be some element in our own consciousness that consents to the hypnotic influence of animal magnetism, the ultimate protection from malpractice is in purifying thought of those traits and beliefs in the conscious and subconscious mind that put us under hypnotic influence. Unless we study Christian Science, we have little or no clue as to the nature of these false elements, and how to be rid of them. When we strive daily to understand God, these forms of animal magnetism are brought to the surface and destroyed. Thought is purified, and we are lifted above the plane where malpractice operates.

We do not emerge out of the dark world of mortal mind into nothing — a vacuum or silent, empty heaven. Actually our life simply keeps getting better. Discord and limitations, little by little, drop away, and we find our life richer, freer, happier, with inexhaustible good constantly unfolding.

This "newness of life" comes about as the law of separation acts again and again to bring us out of the darkness of mortal mind into our oneness with God. Each time we put off personal sense and demonstrate a little more of the Christ-consciousness, we mentally separate ourselves from the malpracticing mentality, and move a little further into the spiritual dimension.

121

As we understand God, we press through the boundaries of the mind, and discover the spiritual realm beyond the senses. Here we find refuge from animal magnetism and its hypnotic influence. It is possible to go so deep into the spiritual realm that malpractice can no longer reach us. This refuge and escape begins right in our present life. We do not leave the mainstream of human life and withdraw from the world to escape animal magnetism. Rather, animal magnetism disappears from our experience and an abundance of good manifests itself right where we are as we progress in Science.

Throughout the ages, men have longed to know this "secret place." Few have ever done so. Even with the discovery of Christian Science — the key to this heavenly kingdom — we still do not understand it. This is because the human mind loves to dwell in the absolute and the idealistic Truth, to theorize on spiritual realities, but it will not handle animal magnetism. If it were possible to achieve this transcending view without handling animal magnetism and malpractice, the world would be much closer to the millennium than it is, and there would be no need to dwell on evil so strongly as we have in this discussion. But in fact, a mighty struggle with all forms of evil is an inevitable part of spiritual progress.

Until we come up against claims that defy healing, we may not be aware of the seeming presence and power of animal magnetism. When we make no effort to handle it, we are not a threat to its hold on us. The fact is, before we begin handling animal magnetism, it is the medium in which we think — the mortal view wherein matter and evil are believed to be realities.

But as we take up the study and treatment, and begin to understand Christian Science, we find that animal magnetism cannot be casually dismissed as 'nothing.' We find a mental force resisting our efforts, both within consciousness and without. To escape its hold on us, we must not only study Christian Science, we must also master the prayer of affirmation and denial. In this prayer

we go beneath the surface of the mind, and begin to rid consciousness of the belief in evil and matter. We bring the truth to bear on
animal magnetism in order to destroy its claims within the heart of
our own consciousness. This spiritualized thought is then immune
to all aggressive mental suggestion.

Most students of Christian Science have experienced
impressive healings, and quite often they have realized such healings by holding to absolute Truth, refusing to admit the reality of the
problem. But when we are healed through this work, we are re-
turning from a sick or abnormal mortal state of mind to a normal
mortal condition. Such healing leaves untouched the material view.
We still have the belief in evil and matter deeply embedded in consciousness, and so physical healing is not a great threat to animal
magnetism. We are as susceptible to malpractice after the healing
as before, for the mind remains very much in the same mortal state.

To go beyond this so-called normal state of mind into a
spiritual understanding of God, we must come to recognize the work
of evil and its use of malpractice, and include in our metaphysical
work specific denials of animal magnetism and malpractice. It is
this denial of evil in all its claims that makes the treatment so unique
and so effective.

It may seem difficult at first to take the initiative and wrestle
with malpractice. It is so much easier to dwell on the idea that God
is Love, and to think about the Truth; but we cannot dislodge the
animal magnetism that has become embedded in consciousness —
the very error that furnishes our consent to malpractice — unless
we bring the Truth to bear on it, and drive it out of consciousness.
As we do this, we make space within for the unfoldment of God's
ideas.

Study and treatment bring about a continuous chemicalization in which the material personality gradually diminishes, and
the spiritual individuality gradually unfolds. As this inner renovation
takes place, we transcend the plane of thought occupied by animal

magnetism, and gradually enter the spiritual realm of Mind. As the nature of God grows ever more distinct and real to us, there is less mortal mind within to provide a channel for malpractice. So the final escape and refuge from malpractice is found in dwelling in spiritual consciousness.

We can achieve this elevated state of mind here and now, for heaven is not far off in some distant time and place. We live in the spiritual realm, and Christian Science is the key to it. Let us then take to heart the angel's message to Daniel: "O man greatly beloved, fear not: peace be unto thee, be strong, yea, be strong."

ABOUT THE AUTHOR: Ann Beals is a life-long Christian Scientist. Her family came into Christian Science through a healing she had before she was a year old. Doctors could not diagnose the illness or cure it. She seemed about to pass on when her mother called in a Christian Science practitioner who prayed for her until she regained consciousness. Within a short time she was completely healed. Her parents then took up the study of Christian Science and the family attended First Church of Christ, Scientist in Louisville, Kentucky. During her early years she had several healings of extremely serious illnesses through reliance on Christian Science. In time her father, Harry Smith, became a Christian Science teacher and lecturer.

While attending Washington University in St. Louis, Missouri, Ms. Beals met and married Robert Beals. They had two sons, Charles and John. After serving the branch church in Decatur, Georgia, in many ways, she became a Christian Science practitioner, listed in *The Christian Science Journal*. She also contributed a number of articles to the Christian Science periodicals.

Early in her practice work, she realized the need for writings that explained more fully how to demonstrate Christian Science. But when she submitted deeper articles to the editors of the periodicals, they were unwilling to publish them.

As she watched the steady decline of the Christian Science Church, her concern for the future of the movement led her, in 1974, to publish independently of the Church organization her booklet *Animal Magnetism*. Because of Church policy, members of the Church, and especially *Journal* listed practitioners, were forbidden to publish writings without the permission of the Christian Science Board of Directors. After publishing her booklet, she was forced to resign her *Journal* listing as a practitioner.

In 1975, she met Reginald G. Kerry. He shared her deep concern about the decline in the Church. His work at Church headquarters in Boston had led him to see that the decline in the Church was largely due to the immorality and corruption at Church headquarters. He delivered an ultimatum to the Board of Directors that they either "clean up things at headquarters" or he would write Church members exposing the corruption and immorality there. When the Board refused to take his threat seriously, he carried out his promise to "write the field." Ms. Beals assisted him in sending the Kerry Letters. For two years, while living in Boston, she worked with him in getting out the first four Kerry Letters. Her book, *Crisis in the Christian Science Church*, tells of these events.

After mailing the fourth Kerry Letter, she moved to California. She resigned from the Church in 1977. She continued assisting the Kerrys in sending out the Letters. In 1980, she started The Bookmark with the conviction that the time had come when deeper writings on Christian Science had to be published and made available to everyone. As this work has progressed, she has been able to publish and promote many profound works on Christian Science that have been suppressed by the Board of Directors over the years.

She presently lives in Santa Clarita, California, where she continues to write papers on Christian Science, and serve as publisher and editor of The Bookmark.

For further information regarding Christian Science:
Write   The Bookmark
Post Office Box 801143
Santa Clarita, CA 91380
Call   1-800-220-7767
Visit our website: www. thebookmark.com